# CRAVE
## CHICAGO

*The Urban Girl's Manifesto*

Melody Biringer

CRAVE Chicago: The Urban Girl's Manifesto

A publication of The CRAVE Company
1805 12th Ave W #A
Seattle WA 98119
206.282.0173

thecravecompany.com/chicago
twitter.com/cravechicago
facebook.com/cravechicago

While every effort was made to ensure the accuracy of the information, details are subject to change so please call ahead. Neither The CRAVE Company nor CRAVE Chicago shall be responsible for any consequences arising from the publication or use.

All editorial content in this publication is the sole opinion of CRAVE Chicago and our contributing writers. No fees or services were rendered in exchange for inclusion in this publication.

Printed in the United States of America

ISBN 978-0-9847143-2-2
Second Edition
December 2011
$19.95 USD

# The Urban Girl's Manifesto

### We CRAVE Community.

At CRAVE Chicago we believe in acknowledging, celebrating and passionately supporting local businesses. We know that, when encouraged to thrive, neighborhood establishments enhance communities and provide rich experiences not usually encountered in mass-market. By introducing you to the savvy businesswomen in this guide, we hope that CRAVE Chicago will help inspire your own inner entrepreneur.

### We CRAVE Adventure.

We could all use a getaway, and at CRAVE Chicago we believe that you don't need to be a jet-setter to have a little adventure. There's so much to do and explore right in your own backyard. We encourage you to break your routine, to venture away from your regular haunts, to visit new businesses, to explore all the funky finds and surprising spots that Chicago has to offer. Whether it's to hunt for a birthday gift, indulge in a spa treatment, take a sewing class or connect with like-minded people, let CRAVE Chicago be your guide for a one-of-a-kind hometown adventure.

### We CRAVE Quality.

CRAVE Chicago is all about quality products and thoughtful service. We know that a satisfying shopping trip requires more than a simple exchange of money for goods, and that a rejuvenating spa date entails more than a quick clip of the cuticles and a swipe of polish. We know you want to come away feeling uplifted, beautiful, excited, relaxed, relieved and, above all, knowing you got the most bang for your buck. We have scoured the city to find the hidden gems, new hot spots and old standbys, all with one thing in common: they're the best of the best!

# A Guide to Our Guide

CRAVE Chicago is more than a guidebook. It's a savvy, quality-of-lifestyle book devoted entirely to local businesses owned by women. CRAVE Chicago will direct you to some of the best local spots—top boutiques, spas, cafés, stylists, fitness studios and more. And we'll introduce you to the inspired, dedicated women behind these exceptional enterprises, for whom creativity, quality, innovation and customer service are paramount.

Not only is CRAVE Chicago an intelligent guide for those wanting to know what's happening throughout town, it's a directory for those who value the contributions that spirited businesswomen make to our region.

Photos by christina noël, except lower left and middle photos by Maureen Schulman

# ShopParty

shopparty.tv, Twitter: @ShopParty

Shoptastic. Unforgettable. One-of-a-kind.
ShopParty produces "the greatest shopping day of your life" experiences for consumer and corporate clients. Bonnie Kaplan, founder and lifelong shopping passionista, works with event planners, concierges, in-house corporate planners and people who just love to shop. From intimate "Shop Like A Star" room-service parties to posh, private client events. If you can dream it, Bonnie can produce it. And you will be wowed!

Bonnie Kaplan

# Q&A

What are your most popular products or services?
My clients call me a "shopping mind reader." I turn their retail dreams and desires into reality. Think one-of-a-kind items created just for you. And I give gifts... lots of gifts.

What is your motto or theme song?
OMG! Where did you get that! Only at ShopParty. Bonnie Kaplan, the self-proclaimed Shopping Ambassador of Chicago, wants to use shopping to make every part of your life great!

What do you CRAVE?
Chocolate, DePaul basketball, costume jewelry, Turner Classic Movies, great chick lit, the admiration of my daughter.

What motivates you on a daily basis?
To bring big business to Chicago.

Deborah Kraemer

 # Q&A

**What are your most popular products or services?**
Our most popular products are our Olive Oil Soaps, Shea Balms and Shea Lips, as well as our soothing bath products like Salt Soaks and Silk Milks.

**What tip would you give women who are starting a business?**
Work hard, have an open mind, stay positive and have fun with your passion.

**What do you like best about owning a business?**
I love the creative process that comes along everyday.

**What is your motto or theme song?**
Each day I come into the shoppe, turn on the music and dance for a few minutes. My motto is from my scuba instruction: Plan the dive, dive the plan.

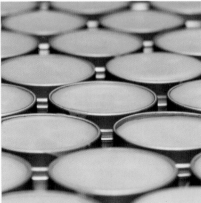

# Abbey Brown
# Soap Artisan

1162 W Grand Ave, Chicago, 312.738.2290
French Market: 131 N Clinton St, Chicago, 312.775.9110
Navy Pier: 600 E Grand Ave, Chicago, 312.595.5543
abbeybrown.com

Local. Handmade. Treasured.
Abbey Brown Soap Artisan handcrafts all-natural bath and body products,
including their signature Olive Oil Soaps, in small batches daily at their
main location in Chicago's West Loop. They also house over 50 local artists
and artisans. Abbey Brown has grown over the years to open locations
at Chicago's Navy Pier and the French Market in Ogilvie Station.

Jessica Swiggum Goldman

# Q&A

**What do you like best about owning a business?**
Creating a place where my employees and customers love to hang out, socialize, get healthy and most importantly have fun!

**Who is your role model or mentor?**
Miss Kellie, my childhood dance teacher. She taught me how to dance, perform and to always carry myself with confidence. Scott Goldman (my husband) and my family for believing in me unconditionally.

**What motivates you on a daily basis?**
Love, fun and friendship. And pineapple... it wakes me up in the morning and gives me the energy to take every day by storm.

# All About Dance

501 W North Ave, Chicago, 773.572.8701
allaboutdance.org

Fun. Inviting. Energetic.
All About Dance is a premier dance studio where kids, teens and adults experience dance in an outrageously fun atmosphere. The kids' program teaches the fundamentals of proper technique while promoting poise, passion and a love for dance. The adult program offers novice and experienced dancers everything from ballet, hip-hop, jazz, wedding instruction and the most popular: cardio dance classes!

# Amy Boyle Photography

312.380.5993
amyboylephotography.com, Twitter: @amyboylephoto

Insightful. Inspired. Engaging.
ABP's keen artistic vision coupled with her genuine and warm personality allow her to
photograph subjects in a way that truly captures their natural essence and is authentic
to each of their personal stories. Her inspired photos and ability to easily connect with
people of all ages bring a unique depth and beauty that rises from every print to tell a tale.

Amy Boyle

# Q&A

**What are your most popular products or services?**
ABP specializes in custom portraiture, PR, theatre and wedding photography. She has been published nationally as well as internationally.

**What motivates you on a daily basis?**
My family. Seeing the world through the eyes of my four sons inspires me to look to the future!

**What is your motto or theme song?**
"Unwritten" by Natasha Bedingfield: "Live your life with arms wide open / Today is where your book begins / The rest is unwritten."

**What place inspires you and why?**
Chicago: for the warmth of its people, strength of its architecture, power of Lake Michigan, and the quiet of the beach on a winter day.

Anne Boyle

# Q&A

**What are your most popular products or services?**
Custom-made medium and large paintings in acrylic and gouache watercolors. In addition, larger diptych and triptych panels in acrylics. All projects are focused on delighting the client.

**What tip would you give women who are starting a business?**
My tip really goes out to women who are thinking about starting a business—it's never too late to make your dream into a reality.

**Who is your role model or mentor?**
My mother. Her support and encouragement are invaluable.

**How do you relax?**
Sitting outside for dinner and a nice glass of vino with my friends and dog, Sasha.

# Anne Boyle Paintings

312.255.8193, anne.boyle@sbcglobal.net, anneboyle.com

Cheerful. Striking. Innovative.
From florals to cityscapes, Anne Boyle's paintings speak to beauty with virtually any subject matter. In addition to her originals, Anne enjoys painting custom artwork for which the client chooses such items as the color palette and theme. Masterful in gouache watercolors, acrylics, and oils, Anne's paintings can be found in some of Chicago's finest homes and at the Andersonville Galleria.

Jacqulyn Hamilton

# Q&A

**What are your most popular products or services?**
Our 60-minute session three-pack is probably our most popular. Folks taking their first steps toward regular self-care try the three-pack en route to plans that support more frequent sessions.

**What tip would you give women who are starting a business?**
Start! Make mistakes and learn your lessons. Allow yourself to be afraid. Use your fear, your excitement, your passion and your intuition to manifest your vision with integrity and intention.

**What place inspires you and why?**
Right now, I'm loving the Garfield Park Conservatory, Harold Washington Library and Fresh Moves Mobile Grocery. They remind me to just be, get curious and problem-solve creatively and resourcefully.

Photos by Bum Bul Bee Photography

# Ashé Therapeutic Massage, Bodywork & Wellness

312.775.2743
ashebody.com, Twitter: @ashebody

Renewing. Alchemical. Holistic.
Ashé specializes in deeply felt work. We bring our services to your home, office or event offering body therapies and wellness support that encourage balance in the body, holistic living and health advocacy. Be it a full body massage, wellness workshop or blog, we provide information and services designed to support and encourage you as you begin or maintain your joyfully, healthy lifestyle.

Photos by Bum Bul Bee Photography

# BabyDolls Boutique

3727 N Southport Ave, Chicago, 773.525.2229
babydolls-boutique.com, pinkandbluearethenewblack.com, Twitter: @BabyDollsBtique

Pinkalicious. Magical. Funtastic.
BabyDolls Boutique is a fun-loving "Magical Queendom" that specializes in unique one-of-a-kind items for mommies, babies and fashionistas. Every girl will discover the BabyDoll in her with their fab-u products! They pride themselves in carrying the top baby products by having five of the #1 sellers in the country. This half baby/half mommy boutique is simply divine!

Vanessa Rodriguez

# Q&A

What tip would you give women
who are starting a business?
Key factor for me would be to never second
guess yourself. If you truly believe in your
product then stand beside it 110%. Do
your research and believe in yourself!

What do you like best about
owning a business?
I'm my hardest critic as my own boss. I take
longer strides and strive more because I
truly believe my boundaries are unlimited.

Who is your role model or mentor?
Credit is due to one of my role models
and former boss, John Syvertsen,
architect—one word: amazing!

What place inspires you and why?
I love Lincoln Park Conservatory or the
Nature Museum to see, smell and breathe,
as these places give me happiness and joy!

Lakeview

Debbie Feiler

# Q&A

**What are your most popular products or services?**
We are known throughout Chicagoland for our layette, christening, classic clothing, and clean and classic nursery items. Our furniture is high-quality with price points to fit any budget.

**What tip would you give women who are starting a business?**
Have a passion for what you do and be hands-on in your business. Never be afraid to ask questions: there is no such thing as a "stupid" question.

**What do you like best about owning a business?**
I like the satisfaction that comes from knowing that this was our idea, and we have built it from the ground up. I also love that I am never bored.

Photos by Julia Franzosa

# Beautiful Beginnings

2163 N Clybourn Ave, Chicago, 773.883.1212
4472 Lawn Ave, Western Springs, 708.246.1212
552 Oakbrook Center, Oak Brook, 630.573.1212
shopbeautifulbeginnings.com, Twitter: @BBeginnings

Happy. Peaceful. Inviting.
Beautiful Beginnings is an upscale, full-service baby boutique offering everything
you need for your new little one. We believe that children are our "greatest
earthly blessings," and we love seeing our customers become a family! At
Beautiful Beginnings, you can find something as simple as a pair of booties
that stay on to something as elegant as a grand armoire for your nursery.

# Beauty on Call

312.335.5350, beautyoncall.com

# Glossed & Found

312.335.5350, glossedandfound.com

# Rodan + Fields Dermatologists

312.335.5350, beautyoncall.myrandf.com

Savvy. Dependable. Award-winning.

Beauty on Call provides beauty and spa services on location for weddings, corporate events and home spa parties. Glossedandfound.com is Stacey Roney's online magazine featuring the best in beauty, fashion and lifestyle. She has also partnered with the biggest names in skincare, Rodan + Fields Dermatologists, and is changing lives by providing award-winning skincare products and the opportunity for independent business ownership.

Photos by Amanda Sudimack, except portrait by Julia Franzosa

## Q&A

**What are your most popular products or services?**
Beauty on Call's popular services are hair and makeup for weddings. The most popular products are Rodan + Fields Anti Aging Skincare and the AMP MD. The results are amazing!

**What tip would you give women who are starting a business?**
Spend time developing and maintaining relationships, giving great customer service and helping others. The word of mouth referrals that result from that goes much farther than paid advertising.

**What is your motto or theme song?**
It's never too late to become what you could have been.

Stacey Roney

ING

What are your most popular
products or services?

" *The Gold Personal Brand
Enhancement Program is our
"best seller." The result for
clients is authentic alignment
of their inside values with
their outside presence.* "

Kali Raoul of The Image Studios

Portrait and lower middle photos by Julia Franzosa

# Bella Bleu

888.420.2030, bellableubridal.com

Couture. Distinctive. Chic.

Featuring designer bridal accessories, Bella Bleu is a couture wedding boutique that has expanded its highly respected online presence with a new boutique location in Park Ridge, Illinois. Bella Bleu captivates brides with luxurious, chic and unique offerings from the world's leading designers and artisans. It is one of a kind, leading the industry as the unrivaled provider of luxury bridal and specialty goods.

 # Q&A

**What are your most popular products or services?**
Bella Bleu features the complete Sara Gabriel Veiling & Headpieces line. Sara's collection of headpieces and veils is meticulously crafted from freshwater pearls, Swarovski crystals, glittering rhinestones and the finest materials.

**What tip would you give women who are starting a business?**
Love what you do! A business with passion and enthusiasm will have the foundation to succeed. Passion sells! Be prepared that it will always "take longer" and cost more!

**What do you like best about owning a business?**
I enjoy evolving my business by embracing change and taking calculated risks. I thrive on knowing that success or failure is a direct result of my efforts.

Andrea Novak

# The Best Career For Me

847.425.9730
thebestcareerforme.com, Twitter: @AltheaMcIntyre

Purposeful. Inspiring. Effective.
The Best Career For Me provides career and executive coaching to clients worldwide. Through 1:1 coaching, private retreats and workshops, clients thrive in their careers by learning how to follow their hearts, leverage their strengths, own their power and work from their soul. The Best Career For Me helps clients achieve their biggest career and lifestyle dreams.

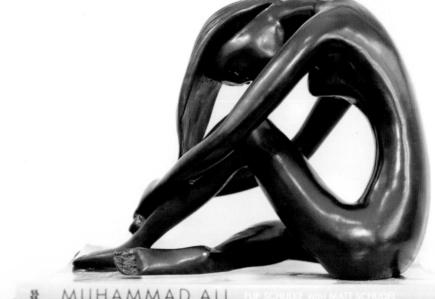

Go confidently in the direction of your dreams! Live the life you've imagined.

-Thoreau

Althea McIntyre

# Q&A

What tip would you give women who are starting a business?
Don't do it alone. Surround yourself with successful business owners. Being in the company and energy of creative entrepreneurs will pay off in ways you'd never imagine.

What is your motto or theme song?
"Go confidently in the direction of your dreams! Live the life you've imagined." —Henry David Thoreau

What place inspires you and why?
I am most inspired when I'm in nature, whether by the lakefront, at the Chicago Botanic Garden or in Jamaica. Nature opens up my creative floodgates.

What do you CRAVE?
Rich and meaningful relationships, good laughter and new adventures.

33

Melissa Lagowski

# Q&A

**What tip would you give women who are starting a business?**
A friend shared this gift with me: "Whatever you can do or dream you can, begin it. Boldness has genius, power and magic in it!" I would pass it on.

**What do you like best about owning a business?**
I love the ability to be present in my children's lives! I still work a TON of hours, but I have flexibility in deciding when I work.

**What motivates you on a daily basis?**
The work we do is very motivational. We have raised almost $2 million for nonprofits in the Chicagoland area and provide unique programs to children in impoverished areas. That's rewarding!

# Big Buzz Idea Group

847.677.8273
bigbuzzideagroup.com, Twitter: @bigbuzzig

Innovative. Meticulous. Versatile.
This Chicago event company works tirelessly to make ideas become reality. Corporations, communities, nonprofits and individuals rely on Big Buzz to produce brilliance on a budget and create memorable events. Big Buzz is dedicated to customizing each project to meet the needs of their clients. They are best known as the trusted team responsible for Ribfest Chicago, which attracts over 55,000 attendees annually.

Eileen O'Neill

# Q&A

What tip would you give women
who are starting a business?
Be organized. Organization is the key to
your success. Don't end your day until you
know what needs to be done for the next.

What do you like best about
owning a business?
Meeting new people: families wanting
to use the service, sitters wanting
to join the service, and fellow small-
business owners. Chicago is a
wonderful community of people.

What motivates you on a daily basis?
I'm constantly asking myself, how can this
be done better? Whether it's my website
or how I communicate with clients—I'm
always looking for ways to improve.

# Blocks Babysitting

312.593.8577
blocksbabysitting.com, Twitter: @blocksbbysttng

Accommodating. Reliable. Essential.
Blocks Babysitting is a babysitting service that provides clients with
babysitters when they need them. Blocks is a one-stop shop for parents:
they cover one-time and recurring childcare needs. All sitters have previous
childcare experience with references and are background-checked. The
team members at Blocks personally meet with families, helping us to
get to know the family and better help with their childcare needs.

Photos by Julia Franzosa

 # Q&A

Rémey Rozin

**What are your most popular products or services?**
Our most popular brands are Iron Fist, Lucky 13, Lux de Ville, Biltwell and Fred Perry. Our most popular services are screen printing and making one-off custom T-shirts.

**What do you like best about owning a business?**
The freedom it gives me to do what I want to do on a daily basis. I get to call my own shots!

**Who is your role model or mentor?**
My dad. He gave me my entrepreneurial spirit.

**What motivates you on a daily basis?**
I love seeing people around town enjoying the items that I know they bought at one of my stores. Daily this drives my desire to grow and expand my business.

Photos by Julia Franzosa

# Broken Cherry Boutique & Custom Apparel

1736 W North Ave, Chicago, 773.278.4000
brokencherry.com, Twitter: @brokencherry

# BC Speed Shop

1734 W North Ave, Chicago, 773.278.4000
bcspeedshop.com

Artsy. Unconventional. Bold.
Broken Cherry Boutique specializes in rockin' clothing, accessories and housewares for women and kids, while the BC Speed Shop specializes in the same kind of items for men. Former roller derby girl Rémey Rozin packs her Bucktown boutiques with clothing and edgy accessories that all revolve around the rock 'n' roll, motorcycle and hot-rod lifestyle.

# Bucktown Pub

1658 W Cortland St, Chicago, 773.394.9898
bucktownpub.com, Twitter: @bucktownpub

Cozy. Lively. Genuine.
Bucktown Pub brings a dose of class to the traditional Chicago corner bar. Family-owned since 2002, regulars and newcomers alike find a home under the traditional tin ceiling or in the secluded beer garden. Weekly trivia and 12 rotating taps give locals a reason to come back, while the attractive bartenders give this bar an air of sophistication.

Piper T. Gorsuch

# Q&A

**What are your most popular products or services?**
We're best known for our 12 taps of mostly local and seasonal craft beer. The hidden gem is our private beer garden. It's the best-kept secret in Bucktown.

**What do you like best about owning a business?**
The best part about owning a business for me is the opportunity to engage with my community and provide jobs to fabulous people. We truly are a dysfunctional family bar.

**What motivates you on a daily basis?**
My customers. They are always part of the conversation when it comes to what's best for Bucktown Pub. I want to provide a place for them to come home to.

Ashbey Riley

# Q&A

What are your most popular products or services?
Family sessions are by far our most popular service. Our clients love that there are no forced poses and that our photos capture their unique family bond and truest personality.

What do you like best about owning a business?
I love knowing that I'm preserving a feeling, that I'm capturing something that can be saved and shared for a lifetime.

What is your biggest fear?
That I'll wake up to find that this whole experience has been just a lovely dream and I have to go back to an office. Some days it's that good.

# Bum Bul Bee Photography

312.841.7427, BumBulBee.com, Twitter: @BumBulBeePhoto

Spirited. Timeless. Vivid.
Bum Bul Bee Photography is a full-service boutique studio located in the heart of Chicago's Old Town. Their mission is simple: to make every session fun, filled with laughter and on good days, lots of gorgeous light. Bum Bul Bee is also dedicated to giving back and recently founded Itty Bitty Rockstars, a directory of local photographers who offer complimentary sessions to NICU families.

Photos by Bum Bul Bee Photography,
except portrait by AdamDaniels.com

# Candyality

3425 N Southport Ave, Chicago, 773.472.7800
The Shops at North Bridge: 520 N Michigan Ave, Chicago, 312.527.1010
Water Tower Place: 835 N Michigan Ave, Chicago, 312.867.5500
candyality.com, Twitter: @candyality

Sweet. Unique. Indulgent.
Right out of the pages of *Charlie and the Chocolate Factory*, Candyality
offers a plethora of everything sweet! Stocking a mouth-watering assortment,
Candyality is derived from the concept of connecting your candy choices to
your personality. Shop one of the many locations of this delightful emporium
and ask the candy specialist what your choices say about you.

# Q&A

Streeterville

**What do you like best about owning a business?**
All of the wonderful people I get to meet. They say that people who love candy are nicer... I would agree!

**Who is your role model or mentor?**
Willy Wonka, of course, because he lives in a world of pure imagination.

**What motivates you on a daily basis?**
The smiles on our customers' and clients' faces. Candy brings out the best in people; they are always happy to be in our stores.

**What place inspires you and why?**
I love malls! They are an enclave of assortment, creativity, movement and buzz.

Terese McDonald

Lakeview

Linda Schmidt

# Q&A

**What are your most popular products or services?**
Family strategy games like Settlers of Catan and Dominion, jigsaw puzzles, games for toddlers like Trucky and Go Away Monster, and yo-yos.

**What do you like best about owning a business?**
After years of working for a slow-moving bureaucracy, I love knowing that if I see something that needs to change in my business, I can make it happen quickly!

**What motivates you on a daily basis?**
I don't view games and puzzles as commodities, I view them as facilitators of fun! When I see people smiling and socializing over a game, I'm in heaven.

Photos by Amy Boyle Photography

# Cat & Mouse Game Store

2212 W Armitage Ave, Chicago, 773.384.4454
cat-n-mouse.com, Twitter: @CatMouseGames

Playful. Unique. Family-friendly.
Since 2007, Cat & Mouse Game Store has been a premier source for games, puzzles, brainteasers and other amusements for kids and adults. Located in Bucktown, they offer a fantastic selection along with friendly assistance with finding the game that's just right for you. From beginning games for toddlers to games for serious strategists, you'll find something for everyone at Cat & Mouse!

What are your most popular products or services?

"*Our practice provides both general and cosmetic dentistry. Porcelain Veneers and Invisalign are two of the most popular treatments we offer. Cosmetic dentistry is incredibly rewarding for everyone involved, it's an amazing feeling to change someone's life with a smile make-over.*"

Dr. Jessica Emery of Sugar Fix (a dental loft)

Sugar Fix (a dental loft) photographed by Julia Franzosa

# TheChainlink.org

773.965.3396
thechainlink.org, w

Environmental. Local. Diverse.
The Chainlink is an interactive website that connects Chicago-area cyclists with each other through user-generated content. With a goal to get people on bikes—individually, together in community and as a movement—The Chainlink wants everyone to ride: with kids, hauling a load, to an exotic destination, with elected leaders or in a really fast race. As of November 2011, the site has more than 6,300 members and receives 50,000 hits a month (in peak season).

Julie Hochstadter

# Q&A

What are your most popular products or services?
As a local social network, cyclists share local information affecting them on the forum, post rides on the calendar, and share photos of their favorite bike and local destinations.

Who is your role model or mentor?
I have many, but those who are respected in the community and raise a family at the same time come to mind first, including Gin Kilgore and Jane Healy.

What motivates you on a daily basis?
How The Chainlink has helped strengthen the cycling community and what we have accomplished. I invite you to join the region's largest cycling network: www.thechainlink.org!

# Q&A

**What are your most popular products or services?**
Branding and print, packaging and digital design.

**What tip would you give women who are starting a business?**
Utilize people and resources around you so that you can focus on what matters most.

**What do you like best about owning a business?**
Working directly with clients and seeing a project through from concept development to completion.

**Who is your role model or mentor?**
My mother who encouraged me as a young child to follow my passion, and my husband for believing in me.

Charisse McAloon

# CharisseM Design

847.204.9229
charissemdesign.com, Twitter: @charissemdesign

Collaborative. Strategic. Detailed.
CharisseM Design, one of Chicagoland's preeminent boutique design firms, brings strategy and creativity together to deliver brand experiences that will engage your audience and develop customer relationships. CharisseM Design's branding, print, packaging and digital work has included an eclectic mix of international brand heavyweights and hometown Chicago favorites: Perrier-Jouët, Target, Kohler, Lana Jewelry, The Land of Nod, Finesse Cuisine, Premier Landscape Contractors and Susan Fredman.

# Q&A

Jessica Zweig and Erica Bethe Levin

**What are your most popular products or services?**
CheekyChicago publishes 30–35 articles a week, hosts events that range from intimate wine-tasting dinners to fashion shows and boasts The Cheeky Card, Cheeky's new state-of-the-art loyalty program.

**What tip would you give women who are starting a business?**
Make sure to cross your t's and dot your i's. Take business seriously; it's hard to be taken seriously in a male-dominated world, so do everything to dispel that stereotype.

**Who is your role model or mentor?**
Our mentor is a woman we met through the Small Business Association named Peg Corwin. Peg is a business advisor counseling start-up businesses. She is an inspiration and a godsend.

# CheekyChicago

cheekychicago.com, Twitter: @cheekychicago

Definitively Bold. Impudent. Saucy.

CheekyChicago is the city's hottest online magazine designed for, by and about the cosmopolitan woman. Featuring dining, nightlife, theater, music, fashion, beauty and beyond, CheekyChicago is your where-to-go guide (with a twist!). Cheeky readers can take advantage of weekly newsletters, exclusive invitations and access to monthly events. Cheeky also boasts their loyalty program, The Cheeky Card, in which readers become VIPs at hot spots all over Chicago.

Valerie Beck

# Q&A

**What are your most popular products or services?**
The tours are popular with bachelorette parties, corporate outings, client entertainment groups and friends out for fun. Chicago Chocolate Tours also offers Chicago Cupcake Tours: all cupcakes, all the time.

**What tip would you give women who are starting a business?**
Follow your heart! I started my business after practicing law. Chocolate was always my passion. You have a gift to share.

**What do you like best about owning a business?**
Owning a business lets me live authentically. My business mission is Uplift Through Chocolate: we uplift our customers, our partner stores, our team and our charity partners.

# Chicago Chocolate Tours

312.929.2939, chicagochocolatetours.com, Twitter: @ChiChocTours

Fun. Fascinating. Uplifting.

Chicago Chocolate Tours provides guided walking and tasting tours to select Chicago chocolate shops, bakeries and cafes. You'll sample the specialties, meet shop owners or artisan chocolatiers and learn about the history and health benefits of chocolate. Depending on the route you select, samples might include Champagne truffles, double chocolate cupcakes, white chocolate bread and chocolate peanut butter crunch bars. The team also provides tours in Philadelphia and Boston. The sweetest tour in town!

Photos by Amy Boyle Photography

Ann Chikahisa

# Q&A

**What are your most popular products or services?**
People are drawn to the organic shape and feel of my jewelry. They like that my pieces are little pieces of art that can become part of their life.

**What do you like best about owning a business?**
The most gratifying part of the business is creating the jewelry and then connecting with the customer. I love getting to know my customers!

**What place inspires you and why?**
I am inspired by nature. When I take my morning walks at the lake, I find so much beauty outside. The perfect petal. The smoothest stone. Unusual organic shapes.

Portrait, lower middle and right photos by Kimberly Postma Photography
main and lower left photos by Erika Dufour

# Chikahisa Studio

773.251.1430
chikahisastudio.com, Twitter: @chikahisastudio

**Bold. Organic. Extraordinary.**
Chikahisa Studio collections are bold, compelling and eminently
wearable. Each piece explores nuances of texture, color and form. Each
design is unique. Each is unlimited in its potential. As remarkable as the
woman who wears them, each piece speaks depth and complexity and
beauty. Inspired by the natural world, Chikahisa Studio's handcrafted
designs fuse effortless styling with a uniquely organic sensibility.

# Content Area Solutions, L3C

773.245.6589
contentareasolutions.us, Twitter: @contentareasol

# N'Side Oluwa's Dream Space

nsideoluwasdreamspace.com, Twitter: @oluwadreamspace

Stimulating. Informative. Collaborative.
Content Area Solutions offers educational experiences for the adult learner.
STEMulating Experiences and Mobile Parent Classroom are some of their specialties.
STEMulating Experiences are fun-filled, Science, Technology, Engineering and
Mathematics activities for adults. How about an ice cream social where you
make your own ice cream? Parents collaborate with other parents for a shared
classroom experience in their homes with the Mobile Parent Classroom.

# Q&A

**What are your most popular products or services?**
STEMulating Experiences, of course. How much fun is it to make a toy that works? Even if you are an adult making slime, it's slimy good fun.

**What tip would you give women who are starting a business?**
Don't be afraid to dream big. Anything is possible, but you have to put your ideas out in the world for the receiver to get them.

**What is your motto or theme song?**
My motto is just breathe... and every now and again relax, relate and release in the words of Whitley Gilbert from "A Different World."

**How do you relax?**
I love to paint. Creating an abstract painting is like creating a window to stars above and all of the dreams that await me.

**What place inspires you and why?**
The Chicago lakefront inspires me. When I walk along the lake, watching the waves, I feel at peace. It is a place to take a break from the hectic day.

**What do you CRAVE?**
Peace, passion and presence in my daily life through STEMulating Experiences.

Oluwafunmilayo Ajayi

Chef Vanessa Moses

# Q&A

**What are your most popular products or services?**
Popular Chicks events are the Cooking Underground dinner-party series and the Will Read for Food food-inspired book club. Both allow for members to be hosts and dishes are shared.

**What do you like best about owning a business?**
The freedom to be creative, no office politics and having my own schedule!

**What is your motto or theme song?**
If you're going to live, *live loud*!

**How do you relax?**
I cook! It's surprising, but I only started cooking three years go (in 2009) when I realized cooking and chopping naturally relaxed me.

# The Cooking Chicks

312.520.6484
thecookingchicks.com, Twitter: @chicookingchick

Passionate. Fun. Food-inspired.

The Cooking Chicks is Chicago's largest organized group of women cooks, chefs, food lovers and eaters! Vanessa Moses, a self-taught home-cook-turned-chef and founder, created the group in 2010 with the purpose of hosting food-inspired events for women. In 2011, The Chick's success led Vanessa to start The Cooking Chicks Cook, a private chef business and food-based event company featuring her personal skills and creations.

Photos by Bohm Bo Bee Photography

Angela Valavanis

# Q&A

**What are your most popular products or services?**
We have five offices in our central quiet zone. Each contains three workstations. Our conference room seats six and is equipped with a telephone (with conference bridge), projector and videoconferencing.

**What do you like best about owning a business?**
I get to set my own hours and work from my dream office. What's not to love? Best of all, I get to share the office with the community.

**What is your motto or theme song?**
Our tagline is "Your Office Home." We provide everything that makes you comfortable at home, plus everything you need in an office setting, so you can be more productive.

# Creative Coworking

By appointment only: 922 Davis St, Evanston, 847.905.1314
creativecoworking.com

Collaborative. Communal. Connective.
Creative Coworking is a members-only work space for creative professionals,
graduate students and entrepreneurs. It is a quiet, comfortable workplace
with a sense of community. Members receive key cards for unlimited
access. Everything you need for work is provided—WiFi, fax machines,
color printers, copiers, scanners—along with some perks like free coffee,
snacks and phone calls. There's even a rooftop deck for working outside!

# Cynthia Ryba

847.989.6979
cynthiaryba.com, Twitter: @CynthiaRyba

Confident. Versatile. Ageless.
As a woman on the go herself, Cynthia Ryba designs pieces that are not only artistically inspiring (whether it be the fabric or silhouette), but also make sense in a modern woman's wardrobe. Through her clothes, her ultimate measure of success is making a woman feel good about herself and comfortable in her own skin.

Photos by Amy Boyle Photography

Cynthia Ryba

# Q&A

**What tip would you give women
who are starting a business?**
If you wait until "the perfect moment" to start
a business, you'll never start a business.
If fear is holding you back: do it afraid!

**What do you like best about
owning a business?**
Creative control. An idea that might seem
irrational in another company may be genius
in mine. I love that I have the final say.

**What is your motto or theme song?**
"Do not conform any longer to the pattern
of this world, but be transformed by the
renewing of your mind." —Romans 12:2

**What place inspires you and why?**
My hometown: Chicago. What we lack
in weather, we more than make up for
in culture, diversity and people. True
Chicagoans are humble and real.

What is your motto or theme song?

*Never quit or give up on your dream. When you know better, you do better.*

Alison Ray of Sassy Moms in the City and
Metropolitan Marketing & Event Group

Sassy Moms in the City and Metropolitan Marketing &
Event Group photographed by Julia Franzosa

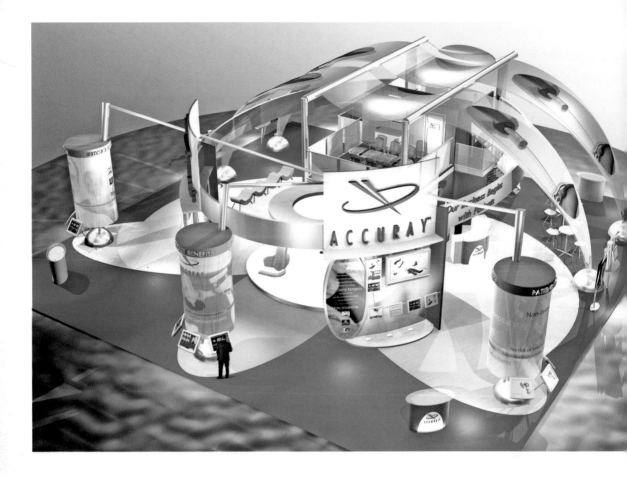

# Dalloo Designs Inc.

773.308.5670
dalloodesign.com

Conscientious. Savvy. Versatile.
Dalloo Design Inc. provides dynamic design services—from fully emersive 3-D exhibits and environments to crisp graphics, renderings and animations. They focus on the latest global design trends to keep customers on the cutting-edge of inspiration.

Annette L. Dalloo

 Q&A

**What tip would you give women who are starting a business?**
Don't let anyone shake your confidence and always follow your passion.

**Who is your role model or mentor?**
My father has been an entrepreneur for as long as I can remember. He inspires me and has always taught me to follow my instincts.

**What is your biggest fear?**
It happened in 2009 when I marketed for six months with no results. It was a scary time for all businesses. However, surviving tough times always makes a business stronger.

**What place inspires you and why?**
I love getting inspiration from my travels. Going to culturally diverse and design-rich cities such as Paris or Barcelona is an integral part of keeping things fresh and innovative.

Elizabeth Wallish

# Q&A

**What are your most popular products or services?**
The Extreme Self Care Six-Month Programs and Corporate Wellness Series Seminars.

**Who is your role model or mentor?**
My daughter is wicked smart. She is unafraid. I admire where she has found herself today at 22. She is honest, kind, determined and passionate! She reminds me who I am.

**What motivates you on a daily basis?**
Our overweight, nutritionally starved, western medicine reliant, inflicted community.

**What do you CRAVE?**
Self-inspired health, financial success, friendships, family, freedom, authenticity and truth.

# Dare 2 Care Now

224.766.9712
dare2carenow.com, info@dare2darenow.com, Twitter: @Walli1E

Holistic. Life-changing. Nutritious.

Dare 2 Care Now is a holistic way of life, providing custom-designed nutrition-driven programs for individuals, teaching them how to eat and what to eat so that they may obtain balance without deprivation. They give the gift of unrivaled health and vitality through accountable coaching and nutrition consulting, thereby introducing whole food living that heals the body.

Dana Frost

# Q&A

**What are your most popular products or services?**
I offer one-to-one coaching, am a workshop creator and facilitator, keynote speaker, spiritual director, Resonance Repatterner©, and I implement around the world coaching trips

**What tip would you give women who are starting a business?**
Don't do it solo. Invite an experienced person to mentor you. Brand and marketing wisdom are essential elements to attracting your clientele, next to having a product people desire.

**What is your motto or theme song?**
You shall know the truth, and the truth shall set you free. Tremendous freedom is experienced when the truth beneath any situation comes to the light.

# DeLightFull Life

danafrost.com, dana@danafrost.com, Twitter: @dana_frost

Intuitive. Authentic. Liberating.
Dana Frost's DeLightFull Life is a boutique-style coaching practice providing multidimensional coaching experiences that heal the broken-hearted, release and reconcile emotional baggage, and identify the strengths and wisdom intrinsic to an individual's body, mind, spirit and intuition. As a Master Certified Life Coach whose experience spans the spectrum of ages, contexts and cultures, Dana designs strategies utilizing core strengths and unites culturally diverse women.

Photos by Julia Franzosa

# the Dorger McCarthy group

By appointment only: Coldwell Banker, 1959 N Halsted, Chicago, 312.867.8138
dorgermccarthy.com

Service-oriented. Reputable. Passionate.

Whether you're in the market to buy or sell a home, the Dorger McCarthy group first and foremost listens... really listens. Understanding your specific needs allows them to provide expert knowledge, targeted strategies and implementation skills in order to reach your goals. Servicing Chicago's lakefront neighborhoods, they are committed to the highest level of service and integrity as they guide you through the purchase or sale of your most prized possession... your home.

Portrait by Oz Images Photography

Sara McCarthy and Julie Dorger

# Q&A

What tip would you give women
who are starting a business?
Follow your passion, create goals,
think big, stay focused but remain
flexible, be organized, *care*, build
balance in your life to prevent burnout,
and lastly, remember to have fun!

What do you like best about
owning a business?
Being able to chart our own course
in developing our business and not
reliving the same day twice!

Who is your role model or mentor?
Pat Coleman, a successful
woman entrepreneur who started
her own business at 72.

What do you CRAVE?
More than 24 hours in a day
to work, play and create!

Adrienne Johns

# Q&A

**What are your most popular products or services?**
Gift bags for holidays, wedding showers and baby showers would be our most popular products. Circles of friends exchange them as their lives move from single to married to married with children.

**What tip would you give women who are starting a business?**
Be your own billboard. Use or wear your product. Let people know what you do. Be ready for the chance encounter that gives you a new idea.

**What do you like best about owning a business?**
Having decision-making responsibility. Success or failure rests with me. In my particular business, I also love the creative side of selecting color stories, patterns and seeing them go "live."

# EcoWrap LLC

847.482.0304
ecowrap.com, Twitter: @ecowrap

Reusable. Timeless. Easy.
EcoWrap designs and manufactures fabric gift wrap called ellaWraps. An ellaWrap reduces paper use and saves time by being easy to use. ellaWraps are cute and stylish. Each one includes a journal that provides a record of each wrap as it passes among family members or friends. They come in a multitude of fabrics and sizes to wrap almost every gift for any occasion.

# eDrop-Off

2117 N Halsted, Chicago, 773.525.7467
1155 N State St, Chicago, 773.525.7467
shopedropoff.com, Twitter: @shopedropoff

Innovative. Convenient. Rewarding.
eDrop-Off is a Chicago-based company that provides luxury consignment services
to style-savvy men and women. Specializing in reselling authentic designer clothing,
handbags, shoes, jewelry and accessories since 2004, eDrop-Off has recycled
nearly 200,000 pounds of clothing. Through an extensive knowledge of the luxury
marketplace and impeccable customer service, eDrop-Off has earned a reputation
as an online power-seller, with more than 150,000 successful transactions.

Corri McFadden

# Q&A

**What are your most popular products or services?**
Free closet consultation and cleaning service, free local pickup in Chicago, free nationwide pickup anywhere in the United States.

**Who is your role model or mentor?**
My mother. She taught me to do what you love and never let an obstacle become larger than yourself. She taught me that I can do anything.

**What motivates you on a daily basis?**
My business. When you wake up and look forward to the day ahead of working with an amazing dynamic staff.

**What do you CRAVE?**
Chicago being recognized on the fashion map!

# Engaging Events by Ali, Inc

773.777.2299
engagingeventsbyali.com, Twitter: @aliphillips

Personable. Organized. Creative.
Ali Phillips of Engaging Events by Ali, Inc—one of Chicago's top wedding consultants—delivers a magical and fun wedding experience to her brides and grooms. Her organization skills, negotiation savvy and appreciation for the "art" of customer service have been invaluable in working with vendors, staying within a budget and creating beautiful, flawless events for her clients.

Main and upper middle and right photos by Glen Abog Photography, upper left photo by Becky Hill Weddings

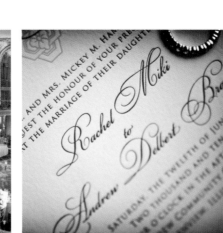

Ali Phillips

# Q&A

What are your most popular products or services?
Most clients book my full wedding planning and design services. I am with the client through their entire engagement to assure that they are on task for a perfect day.

Who is your role model or mentor?
I look up to my parents, who have always taught me to be myself, be friendly and treat everyone with kindness and respect. And to be a mentor.

What motivates you on a daily basis?
I love when you wake up, you have tasks but you also don't know the amazing surprises that life has in store for you. No one day is the same.

Photos by Kristi Sanford of Light on Life Images

# Enliven Couples Therapy

773.469.1507
kimberlysharky.com, Twitter: @kimberlysharky

Innovative. Effective. Dedicated.
Enliven Couples Therapy is a boutique practice devoted to helping the individuals and couples of Chicago live with vitality and cultivate thriving relationships. Kimberly Sharky and her talented associates focus their collective energy on guiding and empowering couples to co-create fulfilling relationships through tailored and confidential therapy as well as workshops on topics including marital preparation, relationship and communication skills, sexual education and intimacy enhancement.

# Q&A

### What are your most popular products or services?
We offer a two-hour Enliven Experience session for couples wanting to spice up or improve an otherwise great relationship and the Weekend Intensive for couples looking to transform their relationship.

### What do you like best about owning a business?
The most fulfilling aspects of owning a business are knowing that there are no limits to what I can accomplish and having the opportunity to employ people I believe in.

### Who is your role model or mentor?
My mentor, Esther Perel, author of *Mating in Captivity*, inspires me to think dynamically, infuses me with zeal and empowers me to be my most powerful and radiant self.

Kimberly Sharky

# Estate Chicago

847.922.5736
etsy.com/shop/estatechicago, Twitter: @estatechicago

Timeless. Recycled. Curated.
Estate Chicago lives and breathes vintage. Kimberly travels the globe to bring her
clients a glimpse of past heirlooms. Estate Chicago specializes in Czech Gablonz glass,
Chicago silver, Arts and Crafts silversmiths and French Gripoix. Estate Chicago exhibits
throughout the Midwest and can be found at Kimberly's favorite show, Randolph Market,
monthly. Check out randolphstreetmarket.com for dates of future events.

Photos by Oz Images Photography

# Q&A

What tip would you give women who are starting a business?
Go big or go home. You get what you put into your business. There never is free time and it takes a strong person to always be "on."

What do you like best about owning a business?
I like calling all the shots, curating the collection, building client relationships, bidding at auction, grabbing a coffee and being at an antiques show all at the same time.

What do you CRAVE?
I love the thrill of the hunt, sourcing the best pieces and offering them to collectors, dealers and appreciative fans of estate jewelry.

Kimberly Oliva

What place inspires you and why?

 *Bloomingdale's: it's my shrine. Seriously, Chicago inspires me. Every time I fly in and they announce 'You're landing in Chicago,' my heart swells. It's the greatest city in the world!*

Bonnie Kaplan of ShopParty

# Evolving Strategies LLC

312.337.8442
evolvingstrategies.com, Twitter: @smschwan

Energizing. Focused. Engaging.
Evolving Strategies LLC is an organizational change management consulting firm helping companies and people learn, adapt and perform. The firm partners with its clients to plan, build and deliver a proactive and systematic approach to deal with change. By engaging the people who will be impacted by the change to understand, accept and commit to the change, clients can mitigate risks and achieve the expected benefits faster.

Sandra Schwan

DON'T
BE AFRAID
TO FAIL.

BE AFRAID
NOT TO TRY.

MICHAEL JORDAN

# Q&A

What are your most popular products or services?
Organizational change management strategy and implementation, organizational change communications strategy and development, leadership development and coaching, large-scale program management, employee engagement, and leadership workshops.

What tip would you give women who are starting a business?
Be passionate about—and be clear on the market for—what you are delivering.

What do you like best about owning a business?
Being able to use my talents and passions to help others further develop their talents and passions.

What is your motto or theme song?
"You Gotta Be" by Des'ree.

What place inspires you and why?
Near water. I find its constant movement and sound to be both calming and inspiring.

What do you CRAVE?
The opportunity to help people become better versions of themselves.

Molly Schemper

# Q&A

What tip would you give women
who are starting a business?
Concentrate on what you do best
and outsource the rest.

What motivates you on a daily basis?
Keeping my clients happy—to see smiles
on the guests' faces is very rewarding.

What is your motto or theme song?
Nine to five (because I wish it were true).

What place inspires you and why?
Lake Michigan (Michigan-side). I grew
up near the lake, and I love swimming;
also, Jamaica: such a great vibe,
good food, music and people.

What do you CRAVE?
Chocolate and peanut butter, spinach
(really, it's true!), good bread and butter.

# FIG Catering

773.793.1035
FIGcatering.com, Twitter: @figmolly

Handcrafted. Inventive. Delicious.
FIG Catering (For Intimate Gatherings) provides handcrafted food and impeccable service for private and corporate gatherings from two to 150 guests. FIG is helpful, fun and inventive in their approach to catering and in-home cooking classes. FIG sources local, organic and sustainable ingredients as much as possible and works with each client to create not only a special event, but a special greener event!

Main and upper right photos by Callie Lipkin Photography, upper left photo by Jen Moran Photography, upper middle photo by Christina Noel Photography, portrait by Amy Boyle Photography

Jeanne Steen

# Q&A

**What are your most popular products or services?**
Figaro's signature collection of authentic vintage fashion illustrations from Paris and NY. Chicago has a long winter, I stock a beautiful assortment of scarves and shawls.

**What tip would you give women who are starting a business?**
Identify what you do best to drive the business and outsource whatever drains you. Ask! Don't shoulder every decision alone. Embrace community. Tap the wisdom around you and stay flexible.

**What do you like best about owning a business?**
Creative freedom. I love the creative process of building something; the last magazine I ran was a start-up! You can craft whatever you imagine.

# Figaro.

A gallery at Vintage Pine, Antiques and Interiors:
904 W Blackhawk St, Chicago, 312.943.9303, vintagepine.com
A gallery at the Andersonville Galleria:
5247 N Clark St, Chicago, 773.878.8570, andersonvillegalleria.com
A gallery at Frankie's on the Park:
2332 N Clark St, Chicago, 773.248.0400, frankiesonthepark.com
A gallery at Julie Watson Style:
900 N Michigan Shops, Chicago, 888.535.0047, juliewatsonstyle.com

figaroantiques.com

Charming. European. Serendipitous.
A terrific resource for original gifts, Figaro evokes a longing for Paris, that
special *je ne sais quoi* that brings beauty and grace into every day. The
owner had spent years at a fashion magazine, and her sensibility is informed
by the European model for a lovely life: mix old and new fashion and home
decor in a singular, unexpected vision—sophisticated, yet approachable.

Erin Krex

# Q&A

**What are your most popular products or services?**
First Class Care's most popular services are nannies, housekeepers and temporary babysitters.

**What tip would you give women who are starting a business?**
I would tell any woman to really network and get the word out. You can save tons of money on advertising by doing what women do best—socialize!

**What do you like best about owning a business?**
I love owning my business because even though I work way more than 40 hours a week, I can take a day off to be with my family if needed.

**What is your motto or theme song?**
Live every day to the fullest!

# First Class Care, Inc.

150 N Michigan Ave, Ste 2800, Chicago, 312.786.9700
3330 Dundee Rd, Ste C2, Northbrook, 847.733.2700
firstclasscare.com, Twitter: @firstclasscare

Professional. Reliable. Attentive.

First Class Care, Inc. specializes in placing exceptional nannies, newborn care specialists, babysitters, housekeepers, house managers, personal chefs and elder care companions. They are a one-stop shop for all your domestic needs. First Class Care has won several awards including 2010 APNA (Association of Premier Nanny Agencies) Agency of the Year and 2010 and 2011 Leading Moms in Business.

Christine Hutchison

# Q&A

**What are your most popular products or services?**
The net shoulder bag that is designed to fit the iPad. Customized pieces such as the "Chicago" embroidered wallets to fit the smartphone are best sellers at Chicago's Midway Airport.

**What tip would you give women who are starting a business?**
Find a similar company that has already paved the way. Research how they are doing it. No need to reinvent the wheel if you know something is working.

**What do you like best about owning a business?**
Creating my own path, leaving my own legacy. Success is not only running a sustainable business but also meeting that triple bottom line and making a social difference.

**What is your motto or theme song?**
"Desserts" is the word "stressed" spelled backward. Take everything in stride, make sure to take the time to have the dessert along your journey.

**What place inspires you and why?**
In Phnom Penh, Cambodia, a young widow is able to provide schooling for her children and needed medical attention through her gainful employment as a seamstress. We are touching lives!

# five ACCESSORIES

Andersonville Galleria: 5247 N Clark St, Chicago, 312.504.3483
fiveaccessories.com, Twitter: @fiveaccessories

Sustainable. Fair-trade. Functional.
five ACCESSORIES is a socially conscious company that features handbags and fashion accessories made from items such as recycled mosquito netting, recycled motorcycle seats and natural coconut shells. Their mission is to empower and deliver sustainable livelihoods for workers and their communities through the sale of eco-friendly and fair-traded, locally made products. Products can be found in the Andersonville Galleria and 100+ nationwide stores.

Andersonville

# Flourish Studios and Studio For Change, PC

3020 N Lincoln, Chicago, 773.281.8140
icanflourish.com, Twitter: @flourish3020

Nurturing. Positive. Imaginative.
Flourish Studios promotes positive change through education, art and
other life-enhancing resources. This urban refuge combines the talents and
expertise of professional therapists along with special events, art exhibits
and merchandise to enrich the lives of children, teenagers and adults. Its
nurturing environment and items are designed to help people flourish.

Julia M. Rahn, Ph.D.

 **Q&A**

What are your most popular products or services?
We provide results-oriented positive psychotherapy for children, teens and adults. In addition, we offer events and merchandise with the mission to help you live your best life.

What tip would you give women who are starting a business?
Dream big but start small. Success builds upon success.

What is your motto or theme song?
We take the PEAR approach to living a great life: promoting Positive change through Education, Art and other life-enhancing Resources.

What do you CRAVE?
A world filled with smiling people.

Jill Salzman

# Q&A

What are your most popular products or services?
Our Founding Moms' Exchanges: monthly, kid-friendly meetups where mom entrepreneurs get together to better build their businesses. It's free to attend and spectacularly informative each and every time.

What do you like best about owning a business?
Satisfaction. There's nothing more satisfying than being your own boss, making up your own rules and having to report to yourself. Oh, and the money? Pretty satisfying, too.

What motivates you on a daily basis?
I'm very motivated by people. I'm very easily infused by people's ideas, interactions and optimism. I've made it my business to help other people build their businesses.

# The Founding Moms

foundingmoms.com, Twitter: @foundingmom

Interactive. Community-oriented. Awesome.
The Founding Moms™ is a collective of local monthly meet-ups where mom entrepreneurs can exchange information, connect, and learn from one another. Incredible women living right in your backyard meet to swap start-up stories, interact with renowned business experts, and build personal and professional connections within the ever-growing network of mom-owned businesses.

# Free To Be

501 W North Ave, Lower Level, Chicago, 312.212.5600
freetobestore.com

Fresh. Friendly. Modern.
Free To Be is a dance and fitness shop that caters to women and children
of all ages. Free To Be offers chic women's apparel that will take you from
your workout to lunch with the girls and beyond. For girls and teens, it
is the ultimate destination for trendy dance essentials. For the tiniest of
dancers, you'll find adorable tutus, skirts and dance accessories.

Trisha Reynolds

# Q&A

**What are your most popular products or services?**
Fresh and fun dance apparel like leg warmers, tanks and tees. Women love our stylish fitness apparel like wraps and leggings that can be worn outside of their workout.

**What tip would you give women who are starting a business?**
Talk to as many people as you can. Other small-business owners are your best resource as they once went through the same thing.

**How do you relax?**
A great workout is the best stress reliever of all. Spinning, dance and yoga are my favorites. I also love to cook for my family and friends.

Old Town

# Gia Claire
# Enterprise, Inc.

312.504.2065
GiaClaire.com, Twitter: @GiaClaire

Empowering. Self-discovering. Authentic.
Gia Claire Enterprise, Inc. is an organization built around a mission statement,
"To empower individuals in a vulnerable state following life changes by enabling
them to face fears through courage, strength and humility." *Head First*, a
memoir, combines the genres of *Eat Pray Love* and *Sex and the City*. Gia is
an author, speaker, columnist and jewelry designer based in Chicago.

Gia Claire

# Q&A

**What tip would you give women who are starting a business?**
Decide what you really want in life. Write down goals and reinforce them daily. Take action and stay true to your vision. Have faith.

**What do you like best about owning a business?**
As the Author of *Head First,* I love the idea of using the written word to affect others. I now have the platform to create and inspire.

**What motivates you on a daily basis?**
Love, and the chance to make a difference to someone.

**What is your motto or theme song?**
One Book. One Day. One Love.

**How do you relax?**
Meditation and Bikram yoga are my religion.

**What place inspires you and why?**
When I am in the city of Chicago, I feel inspired by the energy, the movement and the sound. I feel that I am surrounded, yet isolated.

**What do you CRAVE?**
A life of dreams come true, and the ability to impact others in a positive and significant way.

What are your most popular products or services?

" *Our 60-minute session three-pack is probably our most popular. Folks taking their first steps toward regular self-care try the three-pack en route to plans that support more frequent sessions.* "

Jacqulyn Hamilton of Ashé Therapeutic Massage, Bodywork & Wellness

Nancy Schumacher at Angkor Wat, Cambodia

Meredith Mason at the Equator in Uganda

# Q&A

What are your most popular
products or services?
Our most popular trips include going on
safari in Tanzania, tracking the mountain
gorillas in Rwanda, hiking the Inca
Trail to Machu Picchu and exploring
the archaeological ruins of Turkey.

What tip would you give women
who are starting a business?
Don't be afraid to use your personal
network and connections. It helps to
have strong supporters help spread the
word and get your first few clients.

What place inspires you and why?
Nancy: Traveling to developing
countries puts life into perspective.
I feel incredibly lucky to have the
opportunities I have had and am inspired
by what others make of so very little.

# Global Adrenaline, Inc.

1640 N Wells St, Ste 207, Chicago, 312.863.6300
GlobalAdrenaline.com

Innovative. Responsible. Educational.

Global Adrenaline is a luxury adventure travel company that offers customized itineraries that include unique educational experiences, cultural interactions and socially responsible activities. They work with university alumni associations, affinity groups, individuals and families. They offer trips to over 30 countries around the world including Tanzania, South Africa, Vietnam, Cambodia, Peru, Chile, Argentina, Brazil, Iceland, Turkey, Australia, New Zealand and Antarctica.

Emmy Rigali

# Q&A

**What tip would you give women who are starting a business?**
Love what you do. When it's your own business you'll eat, sleep and breathe it! Don't let anyone tell you it's risky. "Adventure is worthwhile in itself." —Amelia Earhart

**What do you like best about owning a business?**
I love the challenge of bringing in new people to try something they never thought they could do. Then getting them addicted so that they can't imagine not doing it!

**What is your motto or theme song?**
Be yourself... everyone else is taken!

**What do you CRAVE?**
I crave an endorphin rush! Luckily, that's the by-product of my business.

# GO Cycle Studio

501 W North Ave, Chicago, 312.878.4999
gocyclestudio.com, Twitter: @GoCycleStudio

Energetic. Challenging. Exhilarating.
GO Cycle is a creation inspired by Emmy's enthusiasm for life. The classes
embody Emmy's signature brand of cycling: a no-judgment zone of adrenaline-
filled classes with upbeat music guaranteed to inspire you to push harder.

Old Town

Jenn Dieas and Amie Miller

# Q&A

What are your most popular
products or services?
Custom organic airbrush tans,
haircuts and colors.

What tip would you give women
who are starting a business?
Be fearless. Trust your instincts.
Listen often. Enjoy the ride.

What do you like best about
owning a business?
The ability to create your own happiness.

What motivates you on a daily basis?
Our clients inspire us daily to reach
further and take chances. The love and
support they give to us is motivation
to constantly outdo ourselves.

# Golden Girl Chicago

By appointment only: 160 N Halsted St, Ste 3, Chicago, 813.784.4906
goldengirlchicago.com, Twitter: @Goldengirlchi

Adventurous. Creative. Genuine.
Golden Girl Chicago has grown from a girl with a spray gun to a full-on
beauty squad. Golden Girl can beautify you at their West Loop Chicago
location or in the comfort of yours. With genuine and sweet dispositions,
these girls sprinkle sunshine on your dreariest days. From hair and
makeup services to spray tans, they are Chicago's Golden Girls.

# Good Karma Clothing for Kids

224.735.3387
www.goodkarma.co, Twitter: @GoodKarmaSharon

Sustainable. Fashionable. Practical.
Good Karma Clothing for Kids is a subscription clothing service for sizes newborn through 24 months that helps busy, socially conscious mamas choose high-quality, like-new clothes for their little one: clothes that always fit, are always fashionable and always affordable. Parents rave about the convenience of building an adorable wardrobe—and just sending it back for the next size up when baby hits a growth spurt.

Sharon Schneider

# Q&A

**What are your most popular products or services?**
Our Basic Bundle, which offers seven perfect, seasonally appropriate outfits from mom's favorite brands for $27.99 a month. For the cost of just about one new outfit, it's so practical.

**What tip would you give women who are starting a business?**
Avoid naysayers who try to kill your buzz. Hang with other women entrepreneurs and the people who believe in your vision.

**What do you like best about owning a business?**
I love the idea that I'm trying to pursue my vision, rather than implement someone else's. And I'm proud to be a successful role model for my three kids.

# The Green Goddess Boutique

1009 W Armitage Ave, Chicago, 773.281.5600
52 S Washington St, Hinsdale, 630.655.9050
thegreengoddessboutique.com, Twitter: @greengddessbtq

Trendy. Sustainable. Glam.
The Green Goddess Boutique has searched worldwide to bring you the coolest jewelry, hippest handbags and the latest accessories from trend-setting designers who care. They understand the mix and embrace a boho sense of adventure. With their treasure trove of chic apparel, jewelry and handbags, it's easy to be glamorous and green!

Elyce Rembos

# Q&A

What tip would you give women
who are starting a business?
Put in the time and learn every aspect
of your operation. Then delegate and
focus your energy on other areas of your
business, so you can continue to grow.

What do you like best about
owning a business?
There is no limit to what you can achieve.
When it's your own company you can mold
and expand your business to suit your needs
and lifestyle, ultimately creating balance
and harmony in all aspects of your life.

How do you relax?
I'm all about experiences. I love to travel,
explore new places, go out with friends and
spend time with my husband and kids.

Jennifer Moran

# Q&A

**What are your most popular products or services?**
Our 100 percent organic Alpaca knitwear. Specifically, we lead the way in stylish Alpaca knitwear. Using only the finest fiber, our soft-as-cashmere styles are quickly becoming a Chicago favorite.

**What place inspires you and why?**
Bolivia, where I work with our producers. I am inspired by the strength and commitment of Bolivian women to their families.

**What do you CRAVE?**
Consumer understanding of the fashion world. For many, when looking at a clothing tag, there is no understanding of the materials used, who made it, or where it was made.

# GREENOLA Style

Andersonville Galleria: 5247 N Clark St, Mezzanine Level, Chicago, 888.331.0553
GREENOLAstyle.com, Twitter: @GREENOLAstyle

Fair-trade. Sustainable. Fashion-forward.
GREENOLA specializes in sustainable, fashion-forward clothing and accessories.
A Chicago knitwear leader, our GREENOLA line is also featured in over 125
boutiques nationwide. Working directly with women entrepreneurs in marginalized
communities, GREENOLA believes that women have the power to create, nurture
and transform. Each design is a handmade expression of this philosophy, allowing
women worldwide to connect and create a better world through fashion.

Aviva Kleiner

# Q&A

What tip would you give women
who are starting a business?
If you are not a numbers person, find
someone else who is. Make lots of
mistakes and grow each time. Be aware of
limiting beliefs. Make money beautifully!

What is your motto or theme song?
Follow your heart and everything
else will fall into place.

What place inspires you and why?
I find inspiration everywhere. Sometimes it's
as simple as looking through my grandma's
closet, and other times it's unexpected like a
random song that happens to strike a chord.

# Heart Felt

617.359.1608
HeartFeltByAviva.com, Twitter: @AvivaTree

Chic. Creative. Unique.

Heart Felt is a do-it-yourself accessory line that consists of everything from elaborate sequin-beaded fascinators to simple feather headbands and raspberry rockabilly-styled earrings. The designer, Aviva Kleiner, also specializes in custom work for weddings or any special occasion. Every creation is handmade with lots of love and the hopes of inspiring amazing fashion and adding the perfect unique touch to an outfit. Heart Felt believes in giving back to the community and offers internship programs in design, PR, accounting and marketing. In 2012, Heart Felt will be working alongside people with disabilities to continue its mission of shopping with a heart.

Photos by Julia Franzosa

# Helen Ficalora

2014 N Halsted St, Chicago, 773.883.2014
helenficalora.com, Twitter: @helenficalora

Beautiful. Elegant. Personal.
Helen Ficalora jewelry features signature designs that inspire beauty, love and peace.
Helen's collection showcases a stunning assortment of charms, chains, rings, earrings and
bracelets available in solid yellow, white and pink gold and sterling silver. Like the glistening
chandeliers in her magenta jewel box shop in Lincoln Park, her jewelry is often encrusted
with diamonds and gemstones, adding a wonderful sparkle to these golden treasures.

# Q&A

**What are your most popular products or services?**
Alphabet charms, hoop earrings and stacking rings.

**What tip would you give women who are starting a business?**
Do something you love and are passionate about. Learn how to focus and have a strategy for making decisions.

**What do you like best about owning a business?**
Creative freedom and having a platform to assist others.

**Who is your role model or mentor?**
My mother.

**What motivates you on a daily basis?**
Love.

**How do you relax?**
Cooking, being with my family or taking a walk.

**What place inspires you and why?**
Being in nature—whether on the beach or in the woods; I love the inspiration I find around me and it awakens my senses.

Helen Ficalora

# Honey

499 N Main St, Glen Ellyn, 630.469.0000
honeycafe.net, Twitter: @honeymoderncafe

Fresh. Modern. Delicious.
Honey is a neighborhood cafe with a twist. They use quality ingredients like you'd use in your own kitchen. You'll find local natural Dietzler Farms beef, Amish chicken and many organic ingredients. Their organic fair-trade house coffee is locally roasted by Metropolis. There is even an in-house bakery with irresistible treats. Honey makes everything from scratch for super-fresh deliciousness.

# Q&A

**What are your most popular products or services?**
Market Platters: choose three sides from over a dozen fresh choices. Great for people with special dietary needs and for those days when you can't decide on just one thing.

**What do you like best about owning a business?**
The possibilities are endless. It's fun to expand in new ways and watch it grow.

**What do you CRAVE?**
Our "not just" grilled cheese with sweet potato fries. We use artisinal multigrain bread, pesto, arugula and tomatoes melted with cheddar. The sweet potato fries served with dipping sauce are addicting!

Elizabeth Janus

Glen Ellyn

What tip would you give women who are starting a business?

"Be your own billboard. Use or wear your product. Let people know what you do. Be ready for the chance encounter that gives you a new idea."

Adrienne Johns of EcoWrap LLC

Sandee Kastrul

# Q&A

**What are your most popular products or services?**
We believe in the power of communities. Our social media management connects our clients to their customers. We can engage and analyze communication, foster customization of messaging and generate new leads.

**What tip would you give women who are starting a business?**
Dare to dream and hire smart people who think differently than you. Diversity is the primary driver of invention.

**What do you like best about owning a business?**
Creating opportunities for others through process, innovation and people.

# i.c.stars

312.640.3850
icstars.org, Twitter: @icstarsChicago

Connected. Compassionate. Forward.
i.c.stars provides social media management for businesses, allowing
professionals to focus on their core business activities. i.c.stars has developed
a highly effective process that utilizes social media and blogging to create
successful online marketing campaigns. Their social media dashboard analytics
provide deep insights and guidance to their customers as well as strategy to
drive site traffic and leads, which translate into more business for clients.

# The Image Studios

By appointment only: 22 N Morgan, Ste 215, Chicago, 312.421.4660
theimagestudios.com, Twitter: @theimagestudios

Empowering. Comprehensive. Dynamic.
The Image Studios is a decade-old, image communication firm that specializes in personal and corporate branding. Anchored in the premise that "all branding is personal," their dynamic team of presence experts make sure that clients are seen, heard and understood. Boasting hundreds of clients nationwide, TIS is proudly committed to moving great people and exceptional organizations out of the shadows—to change the world.

Kali Raoul

# Q&A

**What are your most popular products or services?**
The Gold Personal Brand Enhancement Program is our "best seller." The result for clients is authentic alignment of their inside values with their outside presence.

**What tip would you give women who are starting a business?**
Regard your best customers, the ones who love the business mission and can afford the product, as valuable partners. Invite their feedback and thank them for it.

**What motivates you on a daily basis?**
Personal growth, my own and that of my team, is the greatest daily motivator. We rise (or fall) together.

Jaclyn Jones

# Q&A

**What are your most popular products or services?**
Yoga Booty Ballet, Zumba, Core Floor and More, Piyo and Bootcamp Ballerinas. These classes provide a hard workout while being engaging and fun.

**What tip would you give women who are starting a business?**
Be patient, it takes a while to learn what your key product/service and demographic are. Things will turn out completely different than you envisioned them, so be adaptive and flexible.

**What do you like best about owning a business?**
People become happier and freer as a result of exercise: they gain self-introspection and self-expression, and it's really rewarding to watch their lives change in front of my eyes.

**What place inspires you and why?**
Maui, Hawaii. It is truly the most magical place I have ever been.

**What do you CRAVE?**
Being healthy and connecting with bright people... and, of course, a new wardobe, lots of spa treatments,travel and the grand slam: a wheatgrass shot combo from Green Corner in Bucktown.

# Indigo Studio

213 W Institute Pl, Ste 704, Chicago, 312.612.9642
theindigostudio.com, Twitter: @IndigoStudio

Inventive. Friendly. Empowering.
Indigo Studio is a fusion fitness studio that hosts inventive and fun classes
catered toward women. Indigoers are instructed to sweat and shimmy their
cares away so that they can rebalance their systems and then go out into
the world as more peaceful, elegant, powerful and sexy women. Located in
River North, the seventh floor loft space is equally tranquil and trendy.

Photos by Bum Bul Bee Photography

# Innovative Orthodontic Centers, PC

By appointment only:
55 S Main St, Ste 251, Naperville, 630.848.6960
111 N Wabash Ave, Ste 1820, Chicago, 312.640.1760
1526 IL Route 59, Joliet, 815.436.8787
OrthoCenters.org, Twitter: @OrthoCenters

Healthy. Relaxing. Fun.
Dr. Ibrahim's passion for orthodontics and her loving approach toward her patients set her apart from the rest. She takes great pride in delivering high-quality orthodontics, utilizing the most innovative, state-of-the-art techniques available. Innovative Orthodontic Centers has proudly won multiple "Best of" awards, voted by their patients and surrounding community.

#  Q&A

What tip would you give women
who are starting a business?
*Go for it!* It was the best thing I ever
did. Have a vision, take the risk, make
it happen. Select amazing people
to go on the journey with you.

What do you like best about
owning a business?
I love being able to practice the way I want
and to treat my patients the way I want.
The sky is the limit, and you are in control.

What is your motto or theme song?
Treat everyone from the heart. Do for
them what you would do for your own
family. Be motivated by doing the right
thing and you will never go wrong.

Dr. Manal Ibrahim LaVacca

# The Insurance People

3419 W Irving Park Rd, Chicago, 773.697.8082
insuranceppl.com, Twitter: @ACEidenberg

**Helpful. Savvy. Insightful.**

The Insurance People takes a fresh approach to helping families and small businesses with their insurance needs. They specialize in educating people about their options and the market, and giving ultimate customer service through unique ideas and above and beyond service. Their fully licensed team is well-versed and ready to take on the most basic to trickiest of requests. They value family, and support small business.

# Q&A

**What are your most popular products or services?**
The Insurance People offers auto, home, business and professional liability, workman's comp, errors and omissions, life, health, disability, long term care and employee benefits insurance.

**What tip would you give women who are starting a business?**
Make sure you have a great lawyer, accountant and insurance agent. You will need them time and time again, and there is no time like the present to be organized.

**What do you like best about owning a business?**
The best part of being a business owner is that all the long hours you work are fun and help *you* reach your dreams and goals, not someone else's.

**What is your motto or theme song?**
"It takes teamwork to make the dream work" and "When the going gets tough, the tough get going."

**What place inspires you and why?**
The beaches of Maine and New Hampshire make me think more clearly, live fully and love passionately. The cold water, sea life and beauty are inspirational.

Alexandra C. Eidenberg

# Jessica Leigh
## Photography and Photo Solutions

312.810.5309, jessicaleighphotography.us, Twitter: @JessicaEntingh
mycmsite.com/jessicaentingh

Expressive. Inspiring. Rewarding.
Jessica Leigh Photography and Photo Solutions offers on-location photography as well as a variety of photo editing, preservation and display products. Jessica believes in honoring your best photos in many different ways. She offers quick, creative solutions for even the busiest people through her Creative Memories business. If you use a camera, she will help identify the perfect way to cherish your photos forever!

Jessica Leigh Entingh

 # Q&A

**What are your most popular products or services?**
The most popular product is StoryBook Creator 4.0. On it, you can create anything from photo books, cards and page prints to custom photo gifts. It has unlimited creative potential!

**What do you like best about owning a business?**
My favorite part of owning a business is actually running it. I love it all—accounting, marketing, sales, design and of course, my photography.

**What motivates you on a daily basis?**
I am motivated by the thrilling feeling I get when I receive a printed digital photo book in the mail. How can I let this feeling be my own?

Julia Franzosa

# Q&A

What tip would you give women
who are starting a business?
Running a successful business takes a lot of
hard work, love and devotion; be ready for it.

What do you like best about
owning a business?
Creative freedom—I love being
able to express myself visually.

Who is your role model or mentor?
Jose Villa, a world-renowned wedding
photographer, has inspired me to
find my own personal style and seek
clients who appreciate my art.

What do you CRAVE?
Real-life connections and friendships. I love
meeting new people and enjoy surrounding
myself with kindness and excitement.

# Julia Franzosa Photography

773.342.1280
julia-franzosa.com, Twitter: @juliafranzosa

Real. Modern. Romantic.
Julia Franzosa Photography, a boutique wedding photographer, is located in Chicago with a modern-romantic documentary style. She focuses on capturing the raw emotion and unscripted moments of your unique day. Beyond your wedding day, Julia also specializes in maternity and newborn photography. Her ability to document the joy of a brand-new life has been enjoyed by many parents.

Photos by Julia Franzosa except portrait by Jen Wright Photography

Amy Lynn Kalas

# Q&A

What do you like best about owning a business?
I love the feeling of personal pride I get every time I complete a successful publishing project or watch someone enjoy a dish I create. And while running a business can involve long hours and working nights or weekends, I truly enjoy the flexibility to have the occasional weekday lunch date, midday yoga class or afternoon jog along the lakefront on a sunny day. Owning a business provides a nice work-life balance.

What place inspires you and why?
Costa Rica's natural beauty—from the beaches to the rainforests and the mountains to the hot springs—calms the mind and inspires passion and creativity. It is one of my favorite countries to visit.

# Just Write! Inc.

773.354.4434, justwritechicago.com

Creative. Meticulous. Personal.

Just Write! Inc. will ensure your websites, articles, blogs, books, educational materials and marketing tools are well-written and flawless. Just Write! has experience with all steps of the writing process—from content creation to fact-checking to proofreading—along with project management experience to ensure your job is done on time and within budget. Amy's passion for words, grammar and all things literary shows in every project she does.

# There's an App for That!

773.354.4434, appetizerforthat.com

Delicious. Crowd-pleasing. Homemade.

There's an App for That! prepares fresh, homemade, crowd-pleasing appetizers, casseroles and desserts for you to heat, serve and pass off as your own! These delectable dishes are presented in cookware that looks like it's right out of your kitchen and can go straight from the oven to your buffet or dinner table. Share your secret or take credit... we'll never tell!

# Q&A

**What are your most popular products or services?**
We work extensively with families that have part-time childcare needs. Our babysitting services are designed to help parents who have occasional requests or set recurring schedules, and/or temporary nanny needs.

**What tip would you give women who are starting a business?**
Focus on something that you love. Create a strong support system. Don't be afraid to make changes to make it work. And be prepared to sacrifice—because it's inevitable.

**What do you like best about owning a business?**
I like the challenge and direct correlation between my efforts and results, but more important is the time I have with my kids and the ability to choose my schedule.

Kayme Pumphrey

# K Grace Childcare

125 S Wacker Dr, Ste 300, Chicago, 773.649.9149
kgracechildcare.com, Twitter: @KGraceChildcare

Convenient. Thorough. Reputable.
K Grace Childcare, a full-service agency that specializes in helping parents with part-time needs, was founded in 2002 with a commitment to placing exceptional childcare providers based on the unique needs of each family. Professional standards, dedication to screening procedures and a focus on providing quality service allow urban families flexibility and peace of mind.

What do you CRAVE?

"Chicago being recognized
on the fashion map!"

Corri McFadden of eDrop-Off

# Killion

1006 W Armitage Ave, Chicago, 773.348.2790
killionclothes.com

Relaxed. Elegant. Effortless.
Killion is a fashion brand and Chicago boutique in the Lincoln Park neighborhood.
The philosophy and aesthetic is about refined simplicity in design, incorporating
clean lines without hard edges. Attention to fit and comfort underscore
every design decision, but modern aesthetics are never sacrificed. Cool,
subdued colors enrich the distinctive cut of the pieces. Accessories from
small, independent designers are chosen to complement the clothing.

 # Q&A

Dana Killion

What are your most popular products or services?
Knit tops of all sizes, shapes and styles. Those great practical but stylish and sexy pieces that can bridge all kinds of lifestyle needs from weekend to work.

What tip would you give women who are starting a business?
Read, study, ask questions. Find a competitor that you can learn inside out. Analyze the heck out of them but when push comes to shove, always trust your gut.

What motivates you on a daily basis?
Change. Discovery. Exploration. If you can't walk down any city street and come up with at least five new ideas, you don't belong in fashion.

# Knickers of Glen Ellyn

492 Main St, Glen Ellyn, 630.469.2727
knickersofglenellyn.blogspot.com, Twitter: @knickersofge

Romantic. Saucy. Warm.
Knickers of Glen Ellyn is an upscale, intimate apparel boutique, offering a lovely selection of personal care items, fun girlfriend gifts and luxurious lingerie, from comfy and cozy to sexy and sophisticated. Knickers specializes in personal customer service and expert bra-fitting. Knickers is the perfect place to host your bridal shower or bachelorette party. They also offer bra fitting parties at your home.

Photos by Bum Bul Bee Photography

Kathryn Hudson

# Q&A

What are your most popular products or services?
Our bra fittings are definitely popular. We offer more than 23 years of experience. We love helping women feel beautiful and confident! It's amazing what the right bra can do!

What tip would you give women who are starting a business?
Follow your heart and be passionate about what you're doing. When you love what you do for a living, it's an amazing feeling!

What place inspires you and why?
I get inspired when I go to New York for the lingerie shows. I love seeing the new collections, talking with other store owners and learning more about this industry.

Photos by Oriana Koren for OKREFOTO

# Koru Street

773.240.2161
korustreet.com, Twitter: @KoruStreet

Eco-friendly. Silly. Colorful.
Koru Street features accessories made with recycled materials from around the world such as bags from festival banners in Barcelona, jewelry from tagua nut in Colombia, wallets from plastic bags and stationery from elephant poo paper in Delhi. Koru Street's goal is to prove that eco-friendly can be fun, colorful or even silly and can go beyond environmental benefits to improve the lives of people worldwide.

# Q&A

**What are your most popular products or services?**
Wallets made from discarded plastic bags by our fair-trade organization in India. In addition to supporting well-paid employment in Delhi, they're lightweight, colorful and no two are ever alike!

**What tip would you give women who are starting a business?**
Make sure it is something you love whole-heartedly. People can sense this when they speak to you, and the sales part of the job is almost effortless.

**What do you CRAVE?**
Traveling the world and seeing it through a million different perspectives.

Amy Stretmater

Amy Butts

# Q&A

**What are your most popular products or services?**
Ladysmith Jewelry is known for transforming vintage chandelier crystals into beautifully handcrafted adornments. We are known for redesigning inherited pieces from grandma into an updated contemporary piece you love wearing daily.

**What tip would you give women who are starting a business?**
You cannot do it alone. Seek other people to help and support you along the way, be organized and have fun!

**What is your motto or theme song?**
Ladysmith Jewelry: adorning the world one beautiful person at a time.

# Ladysmith Jewelry Studio

773.895.8806
ladysmithjewelry.com, Twitter: @LadysmithStudio

Vintage. Reinvented. Timeless.
Amy Butts is a Chicago-based metalsmith, jewelry artist, educator and founder of Ladysmith Jewelry Studio. She gives voice to the found objects she fashions into striking and distinct original jewelry. The daughter of a tool and die worker and a veteran crafter, she is not at all surprised that she makes her living designing and creating. After all, she grew up on Jewell Avenue!

Photos by Bum Bul Bee Photography

# lara miller

847.226.4100
laramiller.net, Twitter: @LaraMiller

Versatile. Smart. Fashion-forward.
Lara's eco-chic pieces have been called "sultry, sophisticated, and as endlessly variable as the woman who wears them" by elle.com. Hand-loomed in Chicago, Lara's work is influenced by the city. Hand-looming is an artisan staple of the collection. Made from sustainable fibers, designs are created with a playfulness that connects to the women who wear them and can be wrapped and flipped, revealing multiple looks.

Main, upper middle and right photos by Helen Burken, portrait and upper left photos by christina noël

Lara Miller

# Q&A

**What are your most popular products or services?**
Our hand-loomed Wear It Your Way™ FLIP™ sweaters! Choose your style, sleeve length, yarn and then color for a customized sweater that can be worn anyway you choose!

**What tip would you give women who are starting a business?**
Believe in yourself and in your idea. The Beatles said it best: "in the end, the love you take / is equal to the love you make."

**What do you CRAVE?**
Health, happiness, and prosperity for me, my family, friends and all in the world. A profitable thriving local company. Clean air. Vegan cupcakes. A sub 4 marathon.

Katherine Darnstadt

## Q&A

**What are your most popular products or services?**
Architectural and interior design services from small renovations to new construction. We donate 10 percent of all fees to provide pro bono design to nonprofits, so every service has a community impact.

**What tip would you give women who are starting a business?**
Failure and fear are the best learning experiences. Have both every day.

**What do you like best about owning a business?**
Flexibility and latitude to collaborate with parallel disciplines to create unique products and experiences while incorporating strong social and sustainable missions.

Photos courtesy LATENT DESIGN, except portrait by Julia Franzosa

# LATENT DESIGN

773.715.7041
latentdesign.net, Twitter: @LATENT_DESIGN

Sustainable. Innovative. Collaborative.

LATENT DESIGN is a full-service architecture and design collaborative whose approach is to realize inventive solutions that turn the constraints of each project into the design trajectory, exploring overlaps between space, program, form, budget and materials. LATENT DESIGN is able to address different project types and clients through a collaborative and sustainable working method based in material research that integrates all creative disciplines.

Main, lower left and lower right photos by Rhonda Holcomb Photography, portrait and lower middle photos by Oz Images Photography.

# Laura Tanner Jewelry

847.563.8858
lauratannerjewelry.com, Twitter: @LTJewelry

Sophisticated. Classic. Inventive.
Laura Tanner Swinand is the founder, designer and maker of Laura Tanner Jewelry
(LTJ). Her distinctive pieces are created to coordinate, so you can mix or match across
her collections. Each design is carefully handmade with gemstones or freshwater pearls
combined with silver or gold-filled chains and findings. Custom and wedding jewelry is
also available. Find LTJ online or at gift shows, galleries, boutiques and museum stores.

# Q&A

**What are your most popular products or services?**
The versatile BonBon Duo necklace, an original design that can be worn six different ways. The unique results from custom jewelry commissions, heirloom redesigns and commemorative birthstone pieces.

**What do you like best about owning a business?**
I always look forward to working in my studio and love setting my own schedule and goals. The satisfaction of creating my own success trumps the challenges of doing so.

**What motivates you on a daily basis?**
I am consistently inspired by seeing women wearing my designs and by hearing from happy clients. Knowing that my jewelry makes someone feel beautiful, confident or generous is so motivating.

Laura Tanner Swinand

Vana Chupp

# Q&A

**What are your most popular products or services?**
Fine arts prints and silhouette jewelry and identity branding for small-scale businesses.

**What tip would you give women who are starting a business?**
Start developing your dream today no matter how unreal it may seem. Make a list of steps toward your goal and accomplish them a day at a time.

**What is your motto or theme song?**
"Every time you smile at someone, it is an action of love, a gift to that person, a beautiful thing." —Mother Teresa

**What do you CRAVE?**
Being part of a group of inspiring women cheering each other up and helping them grow in ways they never thought would be possible.

# Le Papier Studio

847.922.6474
lepapierstudio.com, Twitter: @lepapierstudio

Timeless. Sophisticated. Custom.
Le Papier Studio specializes in elegant silhouette creations. Their charming and intimate custom silhouettes will capture your heart and symbolize your treasured memories for years to come. They work with you to design and illustrate the people, pets and special moments in your life using your photographs.

# The Left Bank Jewelry & Bridal Finery

1155 W Webster Ave, Chicago, 773.929.7422
LeftBankJewelry.com, Twitter: @LeftBankJewelry

Glam. Picturesque. French.
The Left Bank is a Parisian-inspired boutique known for its charming and extensive collection of bridal accessories. Open since 1995, this Lincoln Park boutique remains successful due to creativity, customer loyalty and constant evolution in the bridal market. With the recent addition of the Fancy NY Dress collection, e-commerce and redesigned space, the Left Bank is a must-stop for brides shopping for wedding accessories.

Photos by Julia Franzosa

Susan Metropoulos

# Q&A

What tip would you give women
who are starting a business?
Never stop working to make your business
exactly the way you want it, but be
patient that it won't happen overnight.

What do you like best about
owning a business?
The possibilities are endless in the
direction you can take your own
business—you can always choose a
new path without changing your job.

Who is your role model or mentor?
My grandmother, Genevieve, who
created beauty in everything she
touched. She had an amazing eye for
detail, loved accessorizing and knew
the importance of the finishing touch!

Taxlink Incorporated photographed by Julia Franzosa

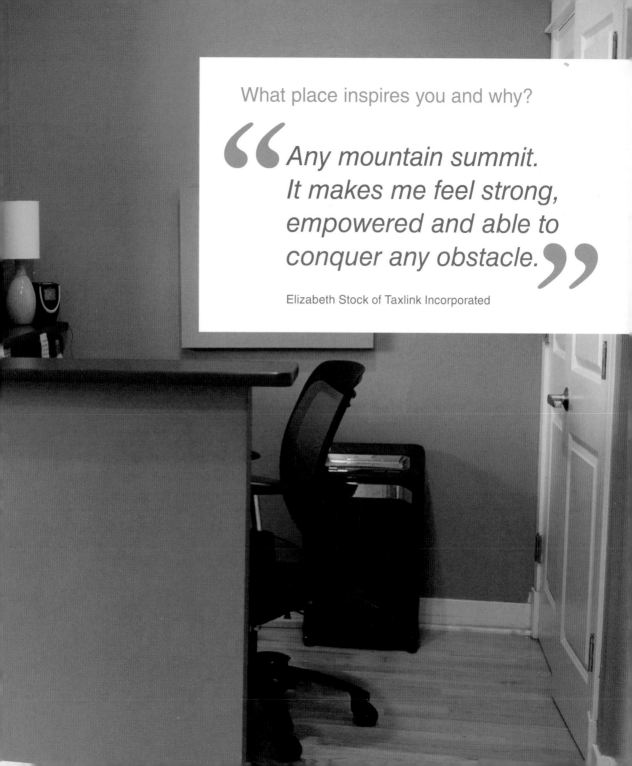

What place inspires you and why?

> *Any mountain summit.
> It makes me feel strong,
> empowered and able to
> conquer any obstacle.*

Elizabeth Stock of Taxlink Incorporated

# LifeStyle
## Physical Therapy & Balance Center

By appointment only: 3130 N Lincoln Ave, Chicago, 773.525.5200
balancechicago.com, Twitter: @balancechicago

Compassionate. Innovative. Bold.
LifeStyle Physical Therapy & Balance Center is a patient-centered clinic. The physical therapists evaluate and treat patients with dizziness and balance disorders. In addition, they use traditional methodologies to treat a variety of orthopedic injuries. Over 90 percent of patients experience a marked decrease in symptoms within four to eight weeks. This passionate group loves to get people back to their optimal health and life.

## Q&A

What are your most popular products or services?
Our most popular service would be vestibular therapy; however, we love working with all injuries.

What tip would you give women who are starting a business?
Follow your passion, break all the rules and define yourself brilliantly.

What motivates you on a daily basis?
My employees: they are a wonderful group of people who make my world a better place. I strive to create an environment that is enriching and supportive for growth.

What place inspires you and why?
Italy. I love the pace, the culture, the food and beauty of the country.

Michele A. Kehrer, PT, DPT, ATC

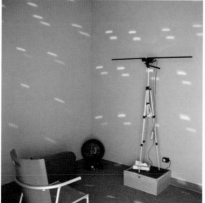

Lakeview

Mana Ionescu

# Q&A

**What tip would you give women who are starting a business?**
Too many people sit on a good idea. Ask for feedback, ask for help, be bold, be brave and get it done!

**What do you like best about owning a business?**
I love that as a small business I can easily choose to use the best technology not the prescribed technology.

**How do you relax?**
I am a passionate scuba diver and nothing relaxes me more than being underwater.

**What do you CRAVE?**
Seeing businesses get excited about talking to people online. It's the age of participation, and I want to see everyone jump in!

# Lightspan Digital

By appointment only: 3701 N Ravenswood, Ste 301, Chicago, 773.442.2448
lightspandigital.com, Twitter: @manamica

Dedicated. Real. Dynamic.
Lightspan Digital is a Chicago digital marketing company that helps businesses make profitable connections through social media and email marketing. The Lightspan team designs, teaches, plans and executes digital marketing. Lightspan takes a hands-on approach to marketing, giving due attention to strategy but stressing the importance of getting things done via strong planning and execution work, thus their motto: "social media done with purpose."

Photo by B.m B. Bee Photography

Photos by Oriana Koren for OKRFOTO

# Lipstic Logic

630.631.7713
lipsticlogic.com, Twitter: @lipsticlogic

Savvy. Professional. Inspired.
Fabulous? Fearless? Finally! Lipstic Logic is a breath of fresh air and a kick in the business butt! Marie Hale Ramos, the visionary behind Lipstic Logic, has the magic marketing touch. Her system of creating duplicate-able, delegate-able and automate-able sales and marketing processes mixed with innovative marketing strategies and soft, nurturing sales patterning gives business owners the most precious gift of all... time to be brilliant.
*Special thanks to The Catalyst Ranch for providing the photo shoot venue.*

Marie Hale Ramos

# Q&A

**What are your most popular products or services?**
Client relationship management systems, sale training, marketing strategies, brand and identity, image consulting, public speaking training and management.

**What tip would you give women who are starting a business?**
Try it. Track it. Change it. If you don't know where your money is coming from, you can't make educated business decisions, delegate processes or control your cash flow.

**What do you like best about owning a business?**
Speed. As a business owner you own your process and the decision making process. Mind you, it's not for the faint of heart. Be the Decision Making Diva. Be Bold.

**What motivates you on a daily basis?**
Abundance. Not just for me and my staff, but collective abundance that lifts others up as we rise. We focus on working with businesses that have an inspired social signature.

**What is your motto or theme song?**
I have been completely inspired by the song 'It's a new day' by will.i.am. "remember its you and me together.'

# Little Independent

littleindependent.com, Twitter: @LitInd

Eclectic. Diverse. Supportive.
Founded in 2010, Little Independent is a Chicago-based online marketplace for sale items at independent retail stores. Its mission is to be an advocate for independent retailers and to give savvy shoppers an easier way to find great independent stores and sale merchandise. Like your favorite retail shopping district, you'll find children's clothing shops, bicycle stores, pet stores and fashion boutiques.

Photos by Oz Images Photography

Lesley Tweedie

# Q&A

**What are your most popular products or services?**
We feature everyone's sale rack in one place. Every item available on Little Independent has been marked down by a shopkeeper at least 10 percent off of its original retail price.

**What tip would you give women who are starting a business?**
Plan your work and then work your plan. If the plan didn't work, try another! Persistence and flexibility are the essential ingredients.

**What do you like best about owning a business?**
It can be stressful, but it is nice to be the decider and to captain your own ship. If we steer off course, it's my job to make things right.

Christy Lucius

# Q&A

What are your most popular products or services?
Our Greek Isle, Mayan Reef, and Hama Rikyu collections are all popular because they are so unique and versatile. And our Sweet Cupcake necklace is big with the baking crowd!

What tip would you give women who are starting a business?
Never give up. You will face rejection and failure, but you'll learn and try again. Those who pick themselves back up and are not afraid to fail build successful businesses.

What place inspires you and why?
Different cultures and countries fascinate me. I will often design pieces after I have been on a trip somewhere or even while looking at books about places I want to visit.

# LUCIUS Fine Jewelry

614.565.3704, luciusjewelry.com

**Handcrafted. Whimsical. Artisan.**

LUCIUS Fine Jewelry is handmade by Chicago jeweler Christy Lucius. Her mission is to create unique yet comfortable jewelry that you will want to wear all the time. Each piece is expertly crafted in either sterling silver or 14kt gold, with only natural gemstones. From gorgeous curving silver to delicate cascading stars, this is jewelry you will treasure for years to come.

Portrait, upper middle and right photos by Amy Boyle Photography, main and upper left photos by Christy Lucius

Saya Hillman

# Q&A

**What tip would you give women who are starting a business?**
Lack of capital is okay. Tell everyone. Ask for and offer help. Have a product people will sell for you. Pay yourself. Barter. Go to things solo. Act confident.

**What motivates you on a daily basis?**
Clients' gratitude. I curate events that help folk connect and challenge themselves, i.e. Fear Experiment: Non-dancers and non-improvisers sign up solo, rehearse with a teacher for three months, and then perform on stage. Round One sold out the 700-seat Park West!

**What inspires you and why?**
Brainstorming sessions with other creatives, and my events. Nothing is more gratifying than seeing relationships form between folks you brought together and hearing laughter from something you produced.

Photos by Richard W. Chapman, except portrait by Kimberly Postma Photography

# Mac 'n Cheese Productions

macncheeseproductions.com, Twitter: @sayahillman

Connecting. Innovative. Infectious.

Mac 'n Cheese Productions started as a videography business. Luckily, "productions" can mean much more than digital media, as it quickly grew a connecting-strangers-to-strangers branch. Now Saya is just as likely to be a name-tag-creator or discussion-facilitator as an editor or videographer, as she helps people expand their networks and themselves. She invites you to check out the variety of opportunities she offers and can't wait to cross paths!

Photos by Carla Englof

# Master Plan by Kathy Codilis

By appointment only: 600 N Lake Shore Dr, Ste 4507, Chicago, 630.862.0228
kathycodilisdesign.com

Warm. Smart. Inviting.

Master Plan is a flat-fee online service that custom designs rooms to scale including furniture, fabrics, drapery, accessories, rugs, paint—everything to complete a dream room. Master Plan is shipped in a fabulous presentation box allowing the client to shop, price and purchase according to his or her budget. Your Master Plan reflects years of experience from a talented Chicago designer at a fraction of the cost!

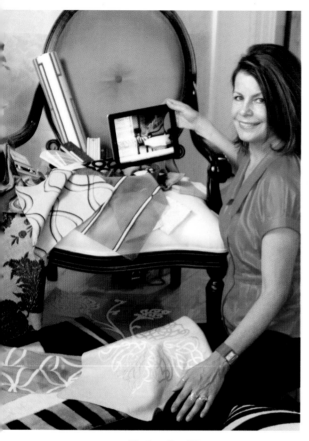

Kathy Codilis

# Q&A

**What do you like best about owning a business?**
That my only boss is my client.

**Who is your role model or mentor?**
My parents—they instilled a sense of integrity in me.

**What is your motto or theme song?**
When in doubt use purple!

**How do you relax?**
A hot bath with salts from the Dead Sea.

**What place inspires you and why?**
The Merchandise Mart. I've spent hundreds of hours there and always find something brilliant!

**What do you CRAVE?**
Chocolate, wine and beautiful fabrics.

# Q&A

What are your most popular products or services?
True ballet technique fitness classes in our Ballerina Evolve™ Series: Ballerina Bum Bootcamp™, Pilates Ball, Ballerina Fight Club™. Regular attendees gain flexibility, poise, strength, grace and lines previously thought unattainable.

Who is your role model or mentor?
Our mother, an entrepreneur herself; she is an operational genius. We try to emulate her selflessness when it comes to serving others; she's all love and brains.

What is your motto or theme song?
Have your "MaZi moment": inspire, dance, achieve!

Marisol Sarabia and Ziba Sarabia Lennox

# MaZi Dance Fitness Centre

1564 N Damen Ave, Ste 208, Chicago, 773.278.9600
mazidancefitness.com, Twitter: @mazidancefitchi, youtube.com/Mazidance1

# MaZi Solutions

By appointment only: 1564 N Damen Ave, Ste 208, Chicago, 773.278.9600
mazidancefitness.com

Powerful. Addicting. Life-enhancing.
MaZi Dance Fitness Centre is a destination for dance enthusiasts featuring
high-energy, results-driven classes ranging from classical training to the
hottest new formats. Their Ballerina Evolve™ classes will change your
body from the inside out and teach you how to activate your muscles
as a dancer. Check out their Ballerina Evolve Workout DVD.

Photos by Bum Bul Bee Photography

Wicker Park

Megan Owdom-Weitz

## Q & A

What tip would you give women
who are starting a business?
Make sure your product is unique and that
it's something people want. If it's something
that you are passionate about, others will
be, too. Be persistent, and don't give up!

What do you like best about
owning a business?
Almost everything! Making my own
schedule, doing different things every
day and being in control of my company's
direction. It's a lot of responsibility,
but the freedom is invigorating.

What motivates you on a daily basis?
My love for art and design, and positive
feedback from my customers and
store owners.

# Megan Lee Designs

773.459.0380
meganleedesigns.com, Twitter: @meganleedesigns

Handmade. Quirky. Hip.
Every Megan Lee Design begins with a pencil drawing that is burnt onto a screen and printed, piece by piece, on her tabletop press. Her cute, one-of-a-kind designs can be found on apparel and greeting cards; they are inspired by her love of animals, nature and the Midwest. Items can be purchased online through etsy or meganleedesigns.com, or at craft shows and independent boutiques.

What place inspires you and why?

"Traveling to developing countries puts life into perspective. I feel incredibly lucky to have the opportunities I have had and am inspired by what others make of so very little."

Nancy Collins Schumacher of Global Adrenaline, Inc.

Elaina Schyb

# Q&A

**What are your most popular products or services?**
Our Marketing Membership benefits any industry: offering design, call center, market research and services all in one place! Clients love it because they choose where energy is focused.

**What tip would you give women who are starting a business?**
Find someone you admire and follow their steps. Surround yourself with like-minded people. Keep an open mind because individuals you meet could take you places you want to go.

**What do you like best about owning a business?**
The results, seeing ideas come to fruition and making clients happy. The freedom to work at midnight or from any café and to meet with clients when they need me.

# Merging Talent

866.637.4366
mergingtalent.com, Twitter: @chgoVixen

Innovative. Direct. Flexible.

Merging Talent is a marketing consulting firm that offers branding and staffing for any business. They come up with creative solutions—staying within budgets while covering all marketing aspects efficiently. A one-stop shop is an asset to any business owner, making magic happen. Merging Talent loves to merge talent—contact them for a complimentary creative consultation.

# MLS ESQ LLC

312.371.2800
mls-esq.com

Mobile. Engaging. Industrious.

If you are a business owner, Meaghan Schneider is the lawyer you might wish you had on staff. She becomes a small part of each business she serves, facilitating the plans of inspired entrepreneurs. Meaghan's focus on the organization, operation, promotion, risk and defense of a business allows that business to focus on what it does best.

 # Q&A

**What do you like best about owning a business?**
Being a business owner can be a limitless outlet for personal and professional growth. Day to day, I work with smart, savvy, strong people who inspire me.

**Who is your role model or mentor?**
My parents are wonderful mentors. I would be fortunate to have my father's business sense and my mother's keen eye and intuition.

**What motivates you on a daily basis?**
The people I work with have heads teeming with genius ideas and hearts brimming with passion for what they do. Their energy and excitement is absolutely stimulating.

**How do you relax?**
It's invigorating to share a belly laugh with my husband and our two kids.

Meaghan L. Schneider

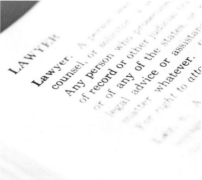

Fosca Shackleton White

# Q&A

**Who is your role model or mentor?**
Maria Montessori. A strong woman who stood by her convictions as an educator until the end of her life, she successfully created an educational philosophy that put children first.

**What is your motto or theme song?**
"By endurance we shall prevail." — family motto of Sir Ernest Shackleton, the British Antarctic explorer. Since my husband is one of his descendants, it's become our family motto, too.

**What do you CRAVE?**
I have a passion for academic excellence. I crave a world where the education of the children is always the first thing we focus on! The children are the future.

# The Montessori Academy of Chicago

1335 W Randolph St, Chicago, 312.243.0977
montessoriacademychicago.org

Warm. Inspirational. Respectful.

The Montessori Academy of Chicago develops every child's natural love of learning. They are proud to provide a prepared environment where our students engage in meaningful work under the guidance of highly trained educators and staff. They understand that not all great minds think alike; they are committed to creating a supportive environment in which each student can reach their greatest potential.

# MP Global Corporation

866.967.0153
mpglobal.net

Dynamic. Personalized. Efficient.
MP Global will help coordinate your company meetings and events. If you have ever held
a meeting, you know how overwhelming managing the logistical details is. MP Global's
experienced team will provide whatever is required to meet your program objectives,
from vendor selection to contract negotiation, registration and travel arrangements.
The goal is to achieve events that are memorable for you and your attendees.

# Q&A

**What tip would you give women who are starting a business?**
Surround yourself with experts to help you (lawyer, accountant, banker). There are many resources for start-up businesses (SCORE, WBDC) that offer great seminars and workshops.

**What do you like best about owning a business?**
I love the flexibility. My hours can be crazy! It's great to be able to work from anywhere and on a schedule that works for me vs. the standard 9am–5pm.

**What is your motto or theme song?**
"Imagine" by John Lennon is my favorite song of all time. My theme song would have to be "On the Road Again" since I travel so much!

**How do you relax?**
I make sure to block off time for one long vacation every year to recharge my batteries.

**What place inspires you and why?**
Italy... it's beautiful and relaxing... and of course, there's the food!

Sue McDonald

Photos by Bum Bul Bee Photography

# Narooma

jennygillespie.com, Twitter: @naroomajenny

Earthy. Expansive. Creative.

Narooma is the label run by Chicago musician Jenny Gillespie. Jenny hopes to expand her roster to female musicians from across the globe. Narooma's first release will be *Belita*, recorded in New York City by Jenny and acclaimed producer Shahzad Ismaily (Tom Waits, Lou Reed, Will Oldham) and featuring Jim White on drums and Marc Ribot on guitar.

## Q&A

**What tip would you give women who are starting a business?**
It takes a while to know how to represent yourself in a marketing sense, especially while trying to create. Stay close to those who champion your work.

**What is your motto or theme song?**
"Only connect." —E. M. Forster

**What place inspires you and why?**
Big Sur—its mysterious and vast landscape combined with a gentle, positive energy in the community.

**What do you CRAVE?**
Women recognizing they can be powerful artists while staying connected to their femininity.

Jenny Gillespie

# The Needle Shop

2054 W Charleston, Chicago
theneedleshop.net, Twitter: @theneedleshop

Inspiring. Nurturing. Communal.
The Needle Shop is a place to be inspired! A DIY sewing school and fabric store,
they specialize in modern print fabrics for fashion and home. Head downstairs
to the classrooms to learn an array of skills with lessons in sewing, upholstery,
screen printing and hand embroidery. TNS focuses on one-session projects,
so you always leave with something completed and entirely show-off-able!

Rachel Epperson

# Q&A

**What are your most popular products or services?**
Sewing 101 is our most popular class and the great equalizer for students starting at different levels. 101 includes zipper installation: the most common sewing fear—obliterated!

**What tip would you give women who are starting a business?**
Don't feel like you have to know everything or have a ton of money to start. Surrounding yourself with other talented people is what will propel you forward.

**What do you CRAVE?**
I crave connection. Ultimately, getting to know people and what makes them tick is what motivates and inspires me.

Jennifer Downing

# Q&A

**What are your most popular products or services?**
It's been exciting to see such interest in DIY classes. Topics like cheese making and preserving are always well attended. A renewed interest in the homemaking arts makes me happy.

**What motivates you on a daily basis?**
Hoping to make a difference in the lives of those with whom I've been privileged to share my passion. I want everyone to eat well and enjoy the process.

**What is your motto or theme song?**
Teaching you to feed those you love.

**How do you relax?**
A cocktail on the patio with good company while the chickens wander the yard.

# Nourish

630.408.9589
nourishcooking.com, Twitter: @nourishcook

Nourishing. Inspiring. Sustainable.
Nourish offers cooking classes to teach you to feed whole food meals to those you love. Seasonally themed classes are small and personal. We continually offer fresh and inspiring cooking opportunities as well as events and trips. Visit and learn to shop a farmers market, make your own sausage or negotiate the grocery store. Nourish is a complete source for sustainable living and homemaking.

Nourhy Chiriboga

# Q&A

**What are your most popular products or services?**
People love the intuitive work that I do, and they let me figure out what might be best for them.

**What motivates you on a daily basis?**
Working with people who are ready for change in their lives. It's satisfying to help create positive, healthy habits and know that you've made an impact in someone's life.

**What is your motto or theme song?**
"You never know" and "as long as you're alive, nothing is ever that bad": I say either of those things to myself at least once a week!

**What place inspires you and why?**
Nature itself. Traveling and seeing how other cultures live. I had the best treatments in Japan. Their culture blends nature into everything.

Logan Square

# Now Studio

By appointment only: 2515 N California Ave, Chicago, 773.276.5278
nourhy.com, Twitter: @nourhy

Affirming. Inspiring. Healing.
Nourhy uses her experience of over 12 years to bring balance and healing
to people with a variety of methods in cozy light-filled Now Studio. Having
been featured in Chicago local press and the show 190 North, she has
garnered a loyal following who flock for her Craniosacral therapy, Reflexology
and unique massage services focused on healing energy practices.

Photos by Oz Images Photography

# Olive.You.Nanny Agency

773.208.3370
oliveyounanny.com, Twitter: @oliveyounanny

Personal. Experienced. Knowledgeable.

Olive.You.Nanny was founded in 2005 by Sarah Davis. Sarah was not only a nanny for several years but also is a mom to three amazing kiddos. Olive.You. Nanny was started to give parents a unique and personal perspective to the nanny-employing business. Olive.You.Nanny has created a method to educate parents so that they feel a connection and understanding with their nanny.

Sarah Davis

# Q&A

What are your most popular products or services?
We offer full-time, part-time, weekend and night nurses.

What tip would you give women who are starting a business?
It's all about research and networking! Then take your time to really get to know the industry and make your company different.

Who is your role model or mentor?
My family. They have always taught me to work hard and play hard. My dad is an extremely hard worker, and I've always admired that.

What motivates you on a daily basis?
All the other moms out there who own their own businesses. It's tough to balance life with a business and a family.

What is your motto or theme song?
Everything happens for a reason. I find myself telling my clients that!

What place inspires you and why?
The city of Chicago. Nothing better than seeing businessmen and -women in the Loop. Something about that thrills me.

What do you CRAVE?
A healthy balance in life. Kids and work can be exhausting, but I make it work.

innovative
ORTHODONTIC
centers

enhancing smiles for life

Innovative Orthodontic Centers, PC
photographed by Bum Bul Bee Photography

What do you like best about owning a business?

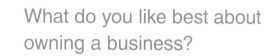

*I love being able to practice the way I want and treat my patients the way I want. The sky is the limit and you are in control.*

Dr. Manal Ibrahim LaVacca of
Innovative Orthodontic Centers, PC

Stacy Ratner

# Q&A

What tip would you give women
who are starting a business?
Create the place in which you most
want to work, for the service you most
want to provide, in the way for which
you most want to be remembered.

What do you like best about
owning a business?
Having the chance to share my lifelong
passion with students, readers,
writers and friends across the city...
and being surrounded by more books
than could ever fit in my house.

What motivates you on a daily basis?
Knowing that in Chicago, a first-class
city in a first-world nation, 53 percent
of adults have limited literacy skills...
and that Open Books is working
to change that for the future.

Photos by Richard W. Chapman

# Open Books

213 W Institute Pl, Chicago, 312.475.1355
open-books.org, Twitter: @openbookstore

Literary. Colorful. Inspiring.
Hailed by the press as "the most beautiful bookstore in Chicago" and
"a rainbow-hued literary Wonka Wonderworld," Open Books is an award-
winning nonprofit emporium where sales of more than 50,000 donated books
in stock (fiction, nonfiction, cookbooks, children's books, and more) support
creative literacy programs for 4,000 kids across the city each year.

# Piccadilly Tea

312.280.1009
PiccadillyTea.com, Twitter: @PiccadillyTea

Unique. Elegant. Delectable.
Piccadilly Tea is a wonderfully unique concept—a tea party catering company that
brings the party to you! Piccadilly Tea provides a quality traditional tea experience
in a relaxing, comfortable atmosphere, whether that be the privacy of your home
or place of business. They have an array of high-quality loose teas, and all of
the delicious scones, breads, tea sandwiches and desserts are homemade.

Photos by Oz Images Photography

Lisa Berens and Meegan Scovell

# Q&A

What is your motto or theme song?
Lisa's favorite quote: "Promise me you'll always remember: You're braver than you believe, and stronger than you seem and smarter than you think." —Christopher Robin to Pooh, A. A. Milne

What motivates you on a daily basis?
The possibility to partner with a customer to create a beautiful environment to entertain in an out-of-the-ordinary way.

What place inspires you and why?
Lisa: London. When I lived there, I first began taking tea and fell in love.
Meegan: Maison Ladurée in Paris and Peninsula Hotel in Hong Kong, both beautiful experiences.

Cassandra Rippberger

# Q&A

**What are your most popular products or services?**
Custom wedding invitations, stationery, notepads and diaper cakes.

**What tip would you give women who are starting a business?**
Believe in your product and what you are doing; there will always be some tedious moments in business but pushing through them is the key to success.

**What do you like best about owning a business?**
Being able to have my dog at work!

**What motivates you on a daily basis?**
The clients. They always send praises and compliments over, and I love seeing their designs come to life just as they imagined.

**What is your motto or theme song?**
To exceed the clients' expectations and "wow" them.

**How do you relax?**
Walking my 140 pound mastiff is surprisingly very relaxing, just a good way to clear my head.

**What place inspires you and why?**
Clothing stores are great places to find new patterns, graphics & design inspiration.

# Pixie Chicago

773.331.4229
PixieChicago.com, Twitter: @PixieChicago

Chic. Fun. Modern.
Pixie Chicago specializes in unique, customized paper designs. In today's
world, where everything is done on the web, it is important to remember
how intimate and wonderful a thoughtful card or note can be. Their goal is to
bring back the personalized touch of a simple piece of mail, whether it be a
handwritten thank-you or an exquisitely crafted special occasion invitation.

Photos by christina noël

Ann Kienzle

# Q&A

What tip would you give women
who are starting a business?
Believe 100 percent in your vision
and your capabilities to execute.

What do you like best about
owning a business?
I think the creative outlet is my
favorite part of owning my store.

What motivates you on a daily basis?
Hearing our customers' excitement (both
young and old) as they walk through
the store motivates me to no end.

What do you CRAVE?
Continued growth and longevity for my
business, continued renewal and progress
for Logan Square and balance for myself.
And pancakes. I love pancakes.

Photos by Julia Franzosa

# *play

3109 W Logan Blvd, Chicago, 773.227.6504
playlogansquare.com, Twitter: @playlogansquare

# The Toy Business

773.489.2575, thetoybusiness.com

Charming. Nostalgic. Enchanting.
*play is a children's toy, book and gift store located in the Logan Square neighborhood of Chicago. Nestled into a historic building in the heart of the square, *play is charming, cozy and fun! *play strives to find unique, creative, and fun playthings for kids of all ages, and after 15 years in the industry, owner Ann Kienzle has done just that! The Toy Business is a boutique consulting firm specializing in the toy and gift industry.

# RAW Marketing

815.410.9139
rawmrktg.com, Twitter: @rawmrktg

Convivial. Progressive. Tenacious.
RAW Marketing strives to set itself apart from others in the industry by focusing on creative and unique marketing strategies for small to mid-sized businesses and entrepreneurs. By staying true to a client's brand and cross-marketing through unique channels to monetize social media efforts, RAW Marketing benefits the marketing efforts of bloggers to remote destination businesses.

# Q&A

**What are your most popular products or services?**
Outsourcing social media management and identity branding are two of our most popular services. Business owners realize that leaving the marketing to the professionals reduces the day-to-day stress.

**What tip would you give women who are starting a business?**
Never lose sight of what you enjoy about your business and who you are: it will get you through days of discouragement and aggravation... because there will be trying days!

**What do you like best about owning a business?**
Having complete freedom to implement creative ideas for my clients and not being constrained by others who do not share my vision or passion for a project.

**Who is your role model or mentor?**
Bethenny Frankel, Ree Drummond and Jen Lancaster have all been on my watch list over the past few years. Dynamic, creative women who have each succeeded, while staying true to themselves.

**What is your motto or theme song?**
Be kind to everyone and yourself. You never know what their day has held... or what the day still holds for you.

Ruth Ann Wiesner

Lisa L. Banks

# Q&A

What do you like best about
owning a business?
I love being able to customize my own
ambience and create my own destiny.

Who is your role model or mentor?
My mother is my greatest gift and my
biggest supporter. She has instilled
in me at an early age, "God bless
the child that has her own."

What motivates you on a daily basis?
The smile I get when I spin my client around,
and she sees her reflection in the mirror.

What is your motto or theme song?
My salon motto is "Balance and Beauty."
I have also loved John D. Rockefeller's
belief: "Gain all you can, save all
you can, and give all you can."

# Red Karma
# Hair Spa and Boutique

2240 S Michigan, Ste 202-203, Chicago, 312.842.DIVA (3482), 312.842.6733
redkarmahairspa.com

## Vital. Communal. Transforming.

Red Karma Hair Spa is an upscale salon dedicated to giving you customized results
in your hair and nail care needs, with a talented team of stylists who believe in the
power of transformation. They really put an emphasis on "when you look better, you
feel better." Set in a relaxing environment, clients can enjoy complimentary snacks
while conversing or walking through the cute boutique filled with affordable luxury.

Photos by Amy Boyle Photography

South Loop

Tai Kojro-Badziak

# Q&A

**What are your most popular products or services?**
Architecture, interior design, space planning, and art selection.

**What motivates you on a daily basis?**
I know that my best work is always ahead of me, and I'm always looking for an opportunity to explore new ideas, textures and spaces.

**What place inspires you and why?**
I always feel refreshed after visiting a different culture—the colors, textures, sights, sounds and scents are always so different; I love bringing those living histories into my work.

**What do you CRAVE?**
Creative projects with energetic clients!

# roomTEN design

312.870.0372
roomtendesign.com

Authentic. Inventive. Comprehensive.

roomTEN design believes that design is life, and they offer architectural and interior design services for clients who want to be engaged in the process and result. They explore your goals to help you define your lifestyle, work flow or particular needs, and then they work closely with contractors, craftsmen and artisans to bring your ideas to life.

Photos by Julia Franzosa

# Sassy Moms in the City

800.320.2289, sassymomsinthecity.com, Twitter: @SassyMomChicago

# Metropolitan Marketing & Event Group

800.320.2289, metromeg.com

Influential. Chic. Sassy.

Sassy Moms in the City (SMITC) is a premier resource dedicated to savvy moms and moms-to-be, featuring the latest fashion and beauty trends, and fitness and lifestyle resources that keep modern moms coming back for more. SMITC readers gain access to The Sassy Scoop newsletter, giveaways, must-have products and invitations to exclusive events. They connect women with resources essential to surviving motherhood with style and sophistication!

*Special thanks to Old Town Social for providing the photo shoot venue.*

 # Q&A

**What are your most popular products or services?**
From integrated media to lifestyle brands to non-profits, savvy businesses leverage Sassy Moms in the City events to engage and connect with our audience of affluent, socially-connected women.

**What do you like best about owning a business?**
Being in full control of developing my brand. Setting my own schedule, having the flexibility to spend time with family and the ability to work from any location remotely.

**Who is your role model or mentor?**
Oprah for her ability to turn her humble beginnings into a thriving business that had such a positive impact on the world for over 25 years.

Alison Ray

Sarah Gullette-Johnson

## Q&A

**What tip would you give women who are starting a business?**
Always know your value. Create systems for processing the business you don't have yet (because it really will come!). Plan for the business you want, not the business you have.

**Who is your role model or mentor?**
My grandfather and brother, Glen, are entrepreneurs in real estate and they, along with my entire family, have been a huge support system for me as I grew this business.

**What place inspires you and why?**
The unique energy and buzz of Chicago is a constant inspiration to me. It has a rich entrepreneurial history, and I feel honored to be part of that tradition.

# SGJ Property Management, Inc.

1732 W Hubbard St, Ste 2B, Chicago, 773.855.2394
chicagolandpropertymanagers.com, Twitter: @SGJPropMgmtINC

Specialized. Community-focused. Trustworthy.
A local Chicago-based association management company, SGJ Property
Management, Inc. focuses on the widely underserved small to midsize communities.
Because they focus exclusively on condo associations, they are able to serve
the unique needs of condo buildings across the city. Their combined education,
experience and technology allow them to provide superior service. SGJ
Property Management, Inc truly brings stewardship to property management.

Wicker Park

THE PRINCESS AND THE PEA

LITTLE RED RIDING HOOD
WILHELM AND JACOB GRIMM | SERIES 15

What do you CRAVE?

*" Seeing businesses get excited about talking to people online. It's the age of participation and I want to see everyone jump in! "*

Mana Ionescu of Lightspan Digital

# Shabazz Law PC

312.962.0324
shabazzlaw.com, Twitter: @shabazzlaw

Professional. Effective. Client-focused.
Shabazz Law PC is a small law firm focusing on business law, intellectual property, minor guardianships and mediation services. Shabazz Law PC takes a client-centric approach to assisting clients with their legal issues. They pride themselves on maintaining a high level of professionalism and integrity as well as providing clients with quality legal services.

Main photo by Zol6z, upper right photos by Amaya S. Jenkins of Thru Her Eyez Photography

Sherese Shabazz

# Q&A

What are your most popular
products or services?
Business law, intellectual property,
guardianships, mediation and bankruptcy.

What tip would you give women
who are starting a business?
Never give up or allow others to tell you
what you cannot do. Do not let other
people's fears become your own fears.
Remove the naysayers from your daily
routine. And, of course, hire legal counsel.

What do you like best about
owning a business?
I like the ability to let all of my creativity
flow, my independence, and that overall
feeling of accomplishing a goal or
making a difference, on my own terms.

Julie Kramer

# Q&A

What tip would you give women
who are starting a business?
Do what you love with love and passion.
Follow your dream with love and passion.

What motivates you on a daily basis?
I am motivated by what I am creating.
This is my dream.

What is your motto or theme song?
As cheesy as it may be, George
Michael's "Freedom."

What place inspires you and why?
Any fabric store. Fabric inspires me: it's
texture, color, design. I love taking a piece
of fabric and bringing it to life in a garment.

What do you CRAVE?
Ease, abundance and happiness,
all while wearing a Shift dress.

# Shift

Andersonville Galleria, 5247 N Clark St, Chicago, 773.544.9128
juliekramershift.com, Twitter: @julikramershift

Simple. Versatile. Soulful.
The Shift brand is for the confident, spirited woman who likes to create her own unique look. Each product is simple and comfortable in design yet has its own unique flair expressed in the detailing. The product line consists mostly of shift dresses but also includes jackets, skirts, bags, scarves and reconstructed sweaters.

Photos by Amy Boyle Photography.

Andersonville

# Shopping Girl XOXO

Available by appointment
517.303.6903, shoppinggirlxoxo.com, Twitter: @shoppinggirlxo

Unique. Customized. Affordable.
Shopping Girl XOXO is a personal shopper and stylist for clients nationwide. With close connections to department stores and "hidden gem" boutiques throughout the Chicago area, it is possible for her to create a valuable and unique experience with each client. Lora enjoys getting to know her clients' personal style and bringing out their best. Shopping Girl XOXO will make you look and feel fabulous!

Photos by Amy Boyle Photography

Lora LaPratt

# Q&A

**What are your most popular products or services?**
Every woman loves to have a wardrobe analysis and shopping lesson. I create flattering and fashionable new wardrobes from existing closets or fantastic new boutiques while pampering my clients.

**What do you like best about owning a business?**
I love what I do! It is an amazing feeling to wake up each morning knowing that I am going to enrich my client's life while having so much fun!

**Who is your role model or mentor?**
Rachel Zoe. She started from just a dream and now has the fashion world at her fingertips with a beautiful group of family and friends surrounding her.

Bela Gandhi

# Q&A

**What tip would you give women who are starting a business?**
Find what you love, and get really good at it. Don't be afraid of the very long hours, rejection or failure. Then, put your spine in and do it!

**What do you like best about owning a business?**
I love having my business for every reason I can think of. Most importantly, it allows unbridled creativity to give clients what they need, and the flexibility to do it.

**What motivates you on a daily basis?**
My energetic, wonderful curious kids who are 7 and 3 years old! Watching my clients have great dates and fall in love. And, my wonderful husband, my greatest cheerleader!

# Smart Dating Academy

312.643.1516
smartdatingacademy.com, Twitter: @SmartDatingAC

Successful. Fun. Effective.
Smart Dating Academy is a nationally renowned date coaching service,
helping singles date smart and find love. Headquartered in Lincoln Park,
they specialize in one-on-one dating coaching, online dating makeovers,
image consulting and relationship assistance. Smart Dating Academy
employs a staff of professional coaches, photographers, hair/makeup artists
and writers to offer singles everything necessary to succeed in dating.

# Soaring Solutions, LLC

773.844.4438
soaringsolutions.net, Twitter: @sue_koch

**Savvy. Strategic. Engaging.**
Soaring Solutions' mission is to prevent businesses from committing random acts of marketing in social media by facilitating strategy development, social platform and etiquette training, and creative content brainstorming. With customized training and ongoing coaching and metrics evaluation, you'll ensure the success of your social media efforts. Social media done right will boost audience and ROI, consume less time than expected, and even be fun!

Sue Koch

# Q&A

**What are your most popular products or services?**
My most popular service is my coaching package. These are hourly sessions used weekly for focused training and strategy, or monthly for ongoing accountability, creative brainstorming and success review.

**What tip would you give women who are starting a business?**
Don't see anything as a failure, but as a lesson strengthening your next success. Take risks. Invest wisely. Don't lose sight of yourself or well-being. Delegate, even if it's laundry.

**What do you like best about owning a business?**
Having no one to blame but myself for "failures" and applauding myself for accomplishing something beyond expectation from the resulting lesson. The fabulously diverse network of professional partnerships I'm building.

**How do you relax?**
Teaching Zumba and PiYo at Indigo Studio. For me, that is relaxing! It's my sanity, clarity, release and physical expression. I crave the energy flows throughout class!

peaking for Conferences, Busin
Organizations & Custom Events

provides customized programs such as keynotes, brea
nized group trainings to facilitate accelerated learning

So Many Social Media Tools, Which do I Choose? Wheth
want a single sign-on, to schedule posts, or have a full syste

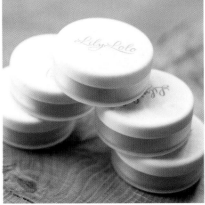

Richelle Ciluffo

# Q&A

What tip would you give women
who are starting a business?
Stay focused, trust the process
and always be grateful.

What do you like best about
owning a business?
Freedom to express myself!

What is your biggest fear?
That I won't be able to keep up
with all my creative ideas.

What motivates you on a daily basis?
The people who say it can't be done.

What is your motto or theme song?
Keep your eyes on the prize.

# The Spa on Oak

67 E Oak St, Ste 3 W, Chicago, 312.280.6283
65 E Oak St, Ste 2, Chicago
www.thespaonoak.com, Twitter: @thespaonoak

# Salon22

1334 Main St, Crete, 708.279.7761
salon-twentytwo.com, Twitter: @salon22Crete

# Face Food

67 E Oak St, Chicago, 708.941.6369
facefood.com

Unique. Sophisticated. Fun.
The Spa on Oak is a beautiful, tranquil spa nestled in the heart of the Gold Coast on the famous Oak Street. Salon22 is a sophisticated salon with cutting-edge talent, providing rock-star service that specializes in hair extensions and color. Face Food is a private botanical skincare line that Richelle created to accessorize her businesses, hoping to expand it nationwide.

# Spilled Ink Press

773.754.7331
spilledinkpress.com, Twitter: @spilledinkpress

Handcrafted. Eclectic. Memorable.
Spilled Ink Press is made up of former architects who now design custom wedding invitations and stationery. Their invitation designs are a marriage of information and form. Each design is handmade, environmentally friendly and customized to give the perfect first impression. Their greeting cards capture a sarcastic voice that reflects down-to-earth humor. Spilled Ink Press embodies the savory and sweet of the stationery world.

Amanda Eich

# Q&A

**What are your most popular products or services?**
"Pocket" wedding invitations are by far what we create for our wedding clients the most. It's the "business in the front, party in the back" invitation!

**What motivates you on a daily basis?**
Specifically, caffeine. Philosophically, reaching my goal of someday being interviewed by either Terry Gross or Craig Ferguson (or both!).

**What is your motto or theme song?**
Think big or go home. There's never been a cliff I didn't jump off of where I didn't find my wings halfway down.

**What place inspires you and why?**
My parent's backyard on a full moon night. It's a quiet and still rural area with stars so big. When the moon is full, it feels like magic.

# Spire Coaching and Consulting

773.398.3696, info@spirecoaches.com
spirecoaches.com, Twitter: @spirecoaches

Personal. Focused. Motivating.
Spire Coaching and Consulting is a full-service coaching organization with many options to meet various client needs. Spire coaches help their clients set excellent goals and then reach those goals quickly by providing strategies, support and structure. Spire clients work with a coach to align their lives with their personal values and priorities, maximizing both their fulfillment and leisure time.

Keri Christensen

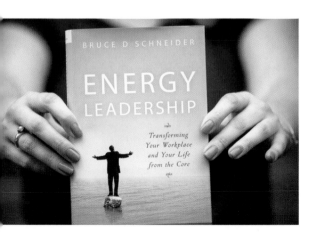

# Q&A

**What are your most popular products or services?**
Weekly one-on-one coaching sessions with a personal coach are Spire's most popular offering, but we also offer energy leadership assessments, group coaching centering on relationship development and time management workshops.

**What tip would you give women who are starting a business?**
When starting your own business, don't get stuck in the planning phase. Find a way to get your feet wet without jumping in over your head.

**What do you like best about owning a business?**
I love designing the programs, materials and services that Spire offers our clients. Also, knowing that I play a part in my clients' success is really motivating!

**What is your biggest fear?**
One coaching principle I live by is that fear signifies opportunity. When you're actively engaged in designing your life, fear can actually be pretty exciting.

**What motivates you on a daily basis?**
There's nothing more important than the relationships we build—that's the true legacy we leave behind.

# Step Brightly
# Creative Group

773.531.3009
stepbrightly.com, Twitter: @stepbrightly

Thoughtful. Witty. Sophisticated.
Offering a full palette of graphic design, web design and marketing services,
Step Brightly creates results that will outshine your expectations. Their goal
is to create deliberate and brilliant design solutions that are meaningful to you
and your business. Step Brightly works with clients in the retail, stationery,
children's branding, event planning and design communities. Their intention is to
communicate clear messaging that will inspire positive change for their clients.

Lisa Guillot

## Q&A

**What tip would you give women who are starting a business?**
Write your inspiration on a Post-it note and look at it every day to remind yourself that the day-to-day hubbub is only a stepping stone to help you reach your goals.

**What do you like best about owning a business?**
I get to design amazing work with fabulous brands and boutiques owned by women who are passionate about what they do. I am constantly inspired by their energy.

**What motivates you on a daily basis?**
Positivity, smiles, soulful house music, glitter, cupcakes, friends, gorgeous fonts, bright colors, giggles, wit and thoughtful conversation.

What motivates you on a daily basis?

*"The clients, they always send praises and compliments over and I love seeing their design come to life just as they imagined."*

Cassandra Rippberger of Pixie Chicago

Pixie Chicago photographed by christina noël

Jessica T. Emery, DMD, PC

# Q&A

**What are your most popular products or services?**
Our practice provides both general and cosmetic dentistry. Porcelain veneers and Invisalign are two of the most popular treatments offered.

**How do you relax?**
Travel is my ultimate relaxation. My best business ideas are often conceived on a sandy beach.

**What is your motto or theme song?**
"Smiling is contagious" has always been my business motto. I feel it's appropriate and applies to more than just dentistry. Give it a try!

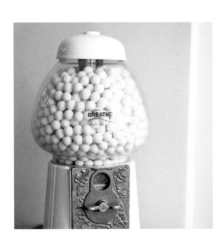

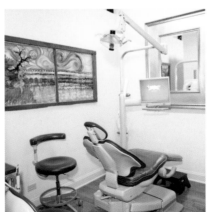

Main, lower left and lower middle photos by Julia Franzosa, portrait and lower right photos by Jon Shaft

# Sugar Fix (a dental loft)

3346 N Paulina, Chicago, 773.883.1818
sugarfixdental.com, Twitter: @sugarfixdental

Fresh. Progressive. Gentle.
Sugar Fix is not a candy store. It's not a guilty temptation at all—but, instead, a dentist's office with a cheeky sense of humor, pink candy-striped logo and a propensity to send clients back out into the world with white, bright smiles.

Lakeview

# Suite Home Chicago

312.638.0891
suite-home-chicago.com, Twitter: @suitehomechi

Luxurious. Convenient. Cozy.
Suite Home Chicago offers luxury temporary accommodations designed to help you make the most of your stay in downtown Chicago. Whether you're here for business or pleasure, their personalized service and attention to detail will make your stay more comfortable. From high-quality bed linens and bath towels to weekly maid service, they've got everything you need to make Chicagoland your home away from home.

# Q&A

What are your most popular products or services?
Furnished apartments in the heart of downtown Chicago. We also can accommodate nationwide as a partner in GO Furnished Housing, a national network of local corporate housing providers.

What is your motto or theme song?
"While moving along toward a dream, may you get lost and find a better one." It encourages me to do better every day and to not be afraid of change.

What motivates you on a daily basis?
Without a doubt, my kids. I not only want to be able to provide for them, but I want to show them what rewards come with some very hard work.

Jennifer Breen

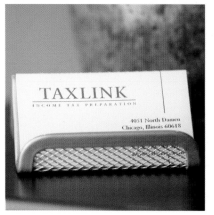

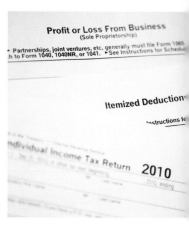

Elizabeth Stock

# Q&A

**What are your most popular products or services?**
Income tax preparation and small business consulting.

**What tip would you give women who are starting a business?**
A solid business plan and detailed bookkeeping are key for success!

**What do you like best about owning a business?**
I love helping people problem-solve, get organized and plan for the future.

**What place inspires you and why?**
Any mountain summit. It makes me feel strong, empowered and able to conquer any obstacle.

# Taxlink Incorporated

By appointment only: 4051 N Damen Ave, Chicago, 773.549.5100
taxlinkinc.com

Energetic. Professional. Affordable.
Taxlink Incorporated is a north side accounting firm serving its clients
in individual and small business income tax preparation and consulting.
Taxlink offers quality service in a relaxed and inviting atmosphere.
Their team of tax professionals consistently keep up-to-date on ever-
changing tax laws, and work hard to help clients save tax dollars.

Photos by Julia Franzosa

# Think Royally Inc

By appointment only: 1200 W 35th St, Chicago, 312.256.7039
thinkroyally.org, Twitter: @thinkoyally

# Sangster Enterprises Inc

By appointment only: 1200 W 35th St, Chicago, 312.857.DAWJ (3295)
dawgelenesangster.com, Twitter: @dawgelene

Purposeful. Collaborative. Savvy.

Think Royally Inc is a nonprofit empowerment organization that focuses on promoting positive change in women and girls through education, networking, leadership development and technology. They build collaborative partnerships to provide inspiration in helping those affected by domestic/sexual abuse and homelessness. They are positively impacting the world of women and girls through mentoring, workshops and life-wellness coaching in Chicago and Miami.

Dawgelene "Dr Dawj" Sangster

## Q&A

**What tip would you give women who are starting a business?**
The key to starting any business is to understand your purpose, why you want to start a business, and then determine if those two things align with your personal/professional values.

**What do you like best about owning a business?**
I enjoy providing a service that I love to those who need/want it and positively impacting the lives of women and girls globally.

**What motivates you on a daily basis?**
My motivation is knowing that I survived life challenges, and now I have an opportunity to positively impact the life of someone else daily.

Bridgeport

# Tiny But Mighty Foods

319.436.2119
tinybutmightyfoods.com, Twitter: @TBMpopcorn

Heirloom. Healthy. Delicious.
Tiny But Mighty features a unique heirloom variety that will change the way you think about popcorn forever. The rare variety of popcorn is a family heirloom passed down for 150 years and perfected by farmer Gene and wife Lynn. It is non-GMO and boasts serious benefits like no hulls to get stuck in your teeth and an unbelievable flavor, reducing the need for unhealthy toppings.

Lynn Mealhow

# Q&A

**What are your most popular products or services?**
We've made it as a company with one product, so it must be good, right? We currently sell un-popped heirloom popcorn which will become the basis for new snack products.

**What tip would you give women who are starting a business?**
There are grants/loans designated for women. Seek assistance from your local Small Business Association to help you find funding. Be patient, nothing happens as fast as you would like.

**Who is your role model or mentor?**
My grandfather has had the biggest impact on my life. He worked with the earth to provide fresh produce for family and friends and wasn't afraid of hard work.

Cassandra Caldwell

# Q&A

**What tip would you give women who are starting a business?**
Believe that you can do it, use your support system and remember that you have failed at 100 percent of the things you don't try.

**What do you like best about owning a business?**
The creative freedom to try something no matter how crazy the idea; knowing full well that I have to own not only the victory but also the failure.

**What motivates you on a daily basis?**
My desire to succeed and to know that I made it happen.

**What place inspires you and why?**
Walt Disney World, the reality of one man with a dream! "It's kind of fun to do the impossible." —Walt Disney

# Trendenzas Inc.

847.975.0134
Trendenzas.com, Twitter: @Trendenzas

Affordable. Trendy. Chic.

Trendenzas Inc. is an online fashion boutique with the hottest accessories at prices too good to believe. Featuring one gorgeous Trend a day at up to 75 percent off, Trendenzas is truly a frugal fashionista's best friend. But move quickly ladies, because Trends are only available for 24 hours. Visit Trendenzas.com and sign up to see a snapshot of today's latest must-haves.

Photos by Kimberly Postma Photography, except lower left photo by Jeff and Lisa-Jo van den Scott

# Tushiya Sweets & Treats

773.234.7141, info@tushiyasweetsandtreats.com
tushiyasweetsandtreats.com, Twitter: @tushiya78

Happy. Heavenly. Delightful.
Tushiya Sweets & Treats creates delicious, sweet experiences through baked desserts and chocolates, all of which are made fresh from scratch using only all-natural and organic ingredients. Whether it is a signature truffle, cake/cupcake, brownie or other sweet, Tushiya provides exceptional quality, taste and service, and leaves people craving their next Tushiya treat.

Ramona S. Thomas

# Q&A

**What are your most popular products or services?**
Our signature truffles, carrot cake, brownies and cupcakes.

**What tip would you give women who are starting a business?**
Believe in what you are doing with every fiber of your being; plan; and surround yourself with people who will both support you and give you honest, critical feedback.

**What is your biggest fear?**
Not living up to Tushiya's name, which is Hebrew for sound wisdom. Everything we do has to be grounded in wisdom.

**What motivates you on a daily basis?**
Every day, I get another chance to live my best life—to make corrections and get better and, hopefully, be a light, inspiration and support to others.

# Urba Baby

1117 W Armitage Ave, Chicago, 773.472.2229
urbababy.com, Twitter: @urbababy

Vibrant. Community-based. Family-oriented.
Urba Baby is a community baby store that offers shopping, classes, workshops
and events to help city families learn and grow. The store carries unique
products that encompass everything needed for a child's day as well as
maternity and nursing accessories. Urba Baby prides itself on offering a wide
range of practical items that have been used and are loved by the owners.

Photos by Julia Franzosa

Marti Goyal

# Q&A

**What are your most popular products or services?**
Westcoast Baby, Chewbeads, Kicky Pants, Ju-Ju-Be, Kula Klips, Zoe Organics and The Tickle Monster Kit. Our monthly story-time, mom and baby yoga and music classes are a hit!

**What tip would you give women who are starting a business?**
Find a balance between work and family, and wake up every day loving what you do. Five steps to success: develop the concept, put it on paper, build a brand, make your idea shine and hire a manager from day one.

**What motivates you on a daily basis?**
My passion for being an entrepreneur, thinking big, making my goals come to life and being the best mom I can be.

265

# Q&A

**What tip would you give women who are starting a business?**
No idea is too small. Even two-inch earthworms can be a business! Get out there, make it happen and learn from those around you.

**What do you like best about owning a business?**
The places it takes you. We have found friends in schools, restaurants, corporations, nonprofits and more. Expanding and learning more keeps us motivated each day.

**What is your motto or theme song?**
When our clients doubt their abilities to care for a population of worms in their home, we happily remind them, "the worms know what to do, just watch and learn."

Stephanie Davies and Amber Gribben

Photos by Blum Bul Bee Photography

# Urban Worm Girl

773.355.4804
urbanwormgirl.com, Twitter: @urbanwormgirl

Sustainable. Educational. Unusual.
Urban Worm Girl shares the wisdom of the red wiggler worms by providing education
and supplies for vermicomposting. Using worms to recycle kitchen scraps and
paper reduces the amount of waste sent to landfills and returns vital nutrients
to the earth. Whether in your home, school or office building, vermicomposting
is a reminder of our interconnectedness to the earth and all its living beings.

Gulf of Mexico

Mississippi

Montessori Academy of Chicago
photographed by Bum Bul Bee Photography

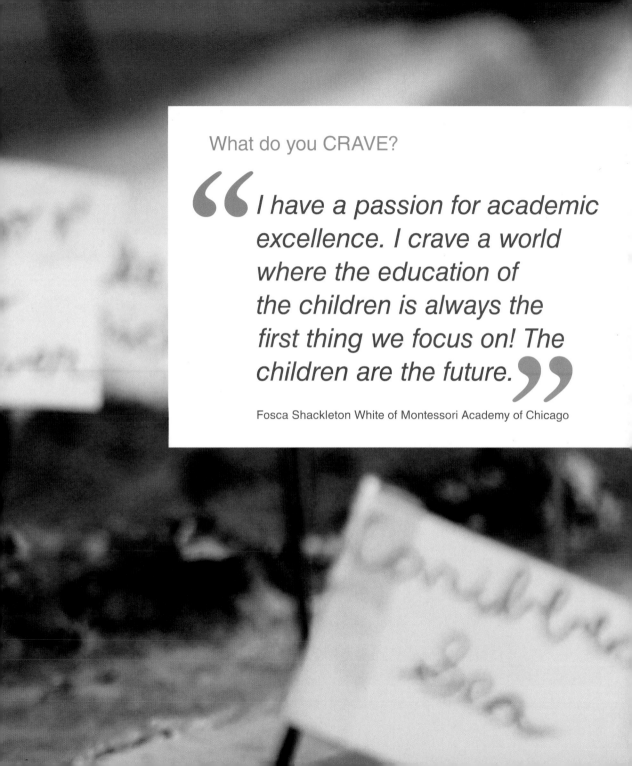

What do you CRAVE?

" *I have a passion for academic excellence. I crave a world where the education of the children is always the first thing we focus on! The children are the future.* "

Fosca Shackleton White of Montessori Academy of Chicago

Charity Gonzalez

# Q&A

What are your most popular
products or services?
The Urban Fitness Warrior monthly
membership includes access to more
than 20 gyms and 500 classes a week
at a monthly fee of $149. The plan is
pay-as-you-go with no contracts.

What tip would you give women
who are starting a business?
If you focus on small steps every day, they
will add up. With action comes traction, and
over time you will feel more empowered
to take on the bigger challenges.

What is your motto or theme song?
Believe in yourself, you are more
capable than you can imagine. If
you think you can, you will.

How do you relax?
Exercise. It is the best stress reliever.

# UrbanFitClubs.com

773.860.2020
urbanfitclubs.com, Twitter: @urbanfitclubs

Strong. Vigorous. Motivating.
Urban Fit Clubs is a gym membership service that gives urbanites access
to a network of the city's most respected boutique gyms and studios with
one affordable and convenient card. Designed for the "urban fitness warrior,"
Urbanfitclubs.com allows members to cross-train, stay motivated with endless
workout options and take advantage of the quality specialty gym experience.

Portrait, main and upper middle photos by christina noël

Main photo and portrait by Julia Franzosa, lower right photos by Prince Agyemang

# Victoria Sdoukos Couture

312.226.9880
victoriasdoukoscouture.com, Twitter: @VSCoutureBridal, v@victoriasdoukoscouture.com

Chic. Glamorous. Innovative.

Victoria Sdoukos Couture, located in the West Loop, offers the bride a truly unique experience. Each appointment is reserved for a personal consultation with Victoria to design a unique and complete wedding-day look. Victoria's boutique features her full line collection of gowns, veils and jewelry that can be customized upon request. The perfect bridal destination for the unique and chic bride. (Formerly Boutique Victoria)

Victoria Sdoukos

 # Q&A

**Who is your role model or mentor?**
My father was a furrier, and with every stitch I make, I feel like I keep his memory alive. I grew up watching him design and learning how to style.

**What tip would you give women who are starting a business?**
You better *love* what you do.

**What do you like best about owning a business?**
I enjoy being my own boss and having the flexibility of expressing myself exactly how I want in my work and designs.

**What do you CRAVE?**
Being the best that I can be. I truly enjoy working with such wonderful women and being a piece of their memorable day!

# Village Paperie & Gifts

2217 W Roscoe St, Chicago, 773.348.7785
villagepaperie.net

Creative. Colorful. Extraordinary.

After 22 years of experience at Original Expressions on Armitage Avenue, the Andrae sisters have come to Roscoe Village. They help brides-to-be customize their dream invitation and fill all their stationery needs, including programs, table cards and thank-you notes. You'll be back in no time for birth announcements!

Frankie Andrae

 # Q&A

**What are your most popular products or services?**
Invitations are the main reason to visit Village Paperie. We specialize in tasteful and hard-to-find christening baptism gifts! And we'll help you find the perfect personalized gift for that hard-to-shop-for person in your life.

**What tip would you give women who are starting a business?**
Meet with as many independent women business owners as you can. Think of it as karma: you'll get back what you put into it—in many ways, much more.

**What do you like best about owning a business?**
Being a part of so many lives and developing long lasting relationships (many turning into friendships). Most come back for birth announcements, christening and 1st birthday invitations.

Monika Porter

# Q&A

What are your most popular products or services?
Brazilian waxing, no-chip manicures and threading services.

What do you like best about owning a business?
The investment of my time and efforts to grow a brand that was once a far-off dream.

How do you relax?
Sunday morning pancakes with my family; my baby boy Chase, my husband Chris and our bulldog Bacardi.

What place inspires you and why?
New York. As an immigrant myself, originally from Poland, I see New York as a monument of the American Dream and Courage.

# Wax On Wax Off

1044 W Taylor St, Chicago, 312.226.1473
waxonwaxoffspa.com, Twitter: @waxonwaxoff

Affordable. Chic. Fun.
Wax On Wax Off is a local, high-end salon offering affordable prices.
Available to support bridal events and private parties or one-stop
shopping—whatever your needs, they've got you covered. Visit their
Taylor Street "little Italy" location (just down from Tuscany).

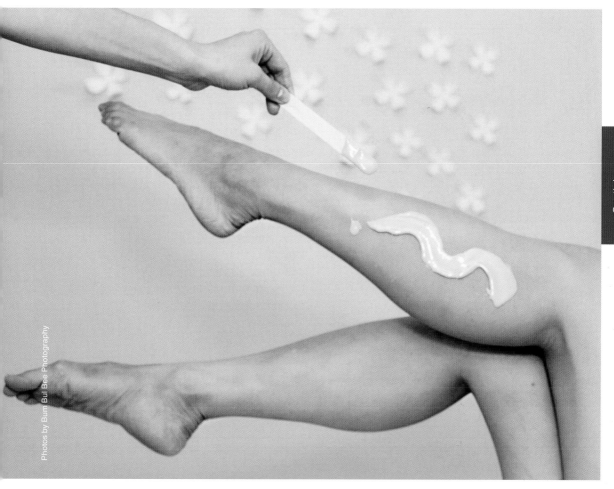

South Loop

Photos by Bum Bul Bee Photography

Linda Olatunde

# Q&A

**What are your most popular products or services?**
Most organizations request marketing plans and my tailored services: Nonprofit communications bootcamp, and Working with You, which is an internal communications seminar teaching corporate employees how to work together.

**What tip would you give women who are starting a business?**
Don't let anyone give you all of the reasons why your ideas will not work without giving you some insight into how it will work.

**What do you like best about owning a business?**
Creating the direction of my company and influencing the industry in a way that hasn't been done before.

**What is your motto or theme song?**
We only go around once, we owe it to ourselves and the people we influence to make sure we are living the life we always envisioned.

**How do you relax?**
I actually teach fitness classes. Zumba and yoga. As I help students find their center, it helps me find mine.

# Yellow Duck PR

312.646.0391
yellowduckpr.com, Twitter: @yellowduckpr

Innovative. Measurable. Personalized.
Yellow Duck PR believes in understanding the whole story and taking a holistic approach to each client's needs. YDPR's approach is to become an expert in their client's industry. The company's mantra is to (1) Define, (2) Organize, (3) Breathe life, and (4) Personalize. "Essentially we make you... You!" YDPR wants each client to appear as though they were the first to ever do it.

# Businesses We CRAVE

Because behind every woman entrepreneur is an entourage of support.

GREAT GUYS, INC.

ggichgo.net

a part-time cto

aparttimecto.com

smilingtoad.net

Lulu B. wine... pairs well with girlfriends!

lulub.com

## TEAMpete

goteampete.com

## SALONBUZZ
### CHICAGO

blog.salonbuzz.com

LICENSED & BONDED

## SKIBOLA

### SERVICES

skibolaservices.com

ARBONNE INDEPENDENT CONSULTANT

Alice Dobrinsky
wonderland.myarbonne.com

# Index

## By Category

# By Category (continued)

# By Category (continued)

# By Category (continued)

# By Neighborhood

# By Neighborhood (continued)

# By Neighborhood (continued)

# Contributors

We believe in acknowledging, celebrating and passionately supporting locally owned businesses and entrepreneurs. We are extremely grateful to all contributors for this publication.

CRAVE Founder

thecravecompany.com
startupjunkie.com

## MELODY BIRINGER

Innovative. Feminine. Connective.

Melody Biringer, self-avowed "start-up junkie," has built companies that range from Biringer Farm, a family-run specialty-food business, to home furnishings to a fitness studio.

Her current entrepreneurial love-child is The CRAVE Company, a network of businesses designed to creatively connect entrepreneurs who approach business in a fresh new way with the stylish consumers they desire. The CRAVE family includes CRAVEparty, CRAVEguides and CRAVEbusiness. What started out as girlfriends getting together for exclusive glam-gal gatherings, CRAVEparty has since expanded into CRAVEbusiness, a resource for entrepreneurs seeking a modern approach, and CRAVEguides, delivering style and substance. Since initially launching in Seattle, Melody has taken CRAVE to more than 30 cities worldwide, including New York City, Boston, Los Angeles, Chicago, Amsterdam and Toronto.

Melody is a loyal community supporter, versed traveler and strong advocate for women-owned businesses.

CRAVE Chicago Partner

macncheeseproductions.com
macncheeseproductions.wordpress.com
Twitter: @sayahillman

## SAYA HILLMAN

Entrepreneurial. Half-full. Contagious.

Saya Hillman is from Evanston, IL, and a Boston College graduate. Saya created Mac 'n Cheese Productions in 2004 and thinks self-employment is the best thing ever! She does video production, teaches digital media to under-resourced Chicago public school students and helps folk make connections via unique, comfortable and fun ways, often with the twist of everyone participating solo. Supper clubs involve folk who want good food and conversation in a laid-back setting. Potluck! is Chicago's finest talking about whatever they want for six minutes each. Fear Experiment allows people who are "bad" at a particular art form to learn said art form and then perform it in front of a sold-out Park West audience. *Smatterings* is an e-newsletter filled with helpful randomness (jobs, grants, activity suggestions, tech insight…). Saya's next wish is to take Mac 'n Cheese outside of Chicago—who has contacts in San Francisco and Amsterdam?!

# Contributors (continued)

**Alison Turner**
*graphic designer*
alisonjturner.com

Alison is a passionate designer and critical thinker from Seattle. She supports human rights and the local food movement. She enjoys researching interesting things, volunteering, being outside, dancing, cooking and running.

**Amanda Buzard**
*lead designer*
amandabuzard.com

Amanda is a Seattle native inspired by clean patterns and vintage design. She chases many creative and active pursuits in her spare time, including photography, baking, attempting DIY projects and exploring the beautiful Pacific Northwest.

**Lilla Kovacs**
*operations manager*
lilla@thecravecompany.com

As the operations manager, Lilla ensures that everything runs like clockwork. In her limited spare time, she enjoys baking, shoe shopping, traveling, art, Apple products and daydreaming about her hometowns, Arad, Romania and Tel-Aviv, Israel.

**Mollie Ruiz-Hopper**
*social media director*
mollie@thecravecompany.com
mollieinseattle.com

A Seattle native, Mollie enjoys nothing more than walking through downtown in high heels with a latte in one hand and her cell phone in the other. She is inspired by CRAVE and is slightly obsessed with social media.

**Nicole Shema**
*project manager*
nicole@thecravecompany.com

A Seattle native, Nicole is happy to be back in her city after graduating from the University of Oregon in 2009. Nicole has a passion for travel, and she loves discovering new places around Seattle with friends, running, shopping, and reading in coffee shops.

**Carrie Wicks**
*copy editor*
linkedin.com/in/carriewicks

Carrie has been proofreading professionally for 14-plus years in mostly creative fields. When she's not proofreading or copyediting, she's reading, singing jazz, walking in the woods or gardening.

### Lesley de Leon
*project manager*
linkedln/in/lesleydeleon

Lesley is on the road less traveled. With a MBA, she is interested in marketing, promotions, events, entertainment, and social media. Lesley loves traveling, baking, taking photos and finding new places to eat and explore.

### Adam Daniels A.S.M.P.
*photographer*
adamdaniels.com, 312.504.0728
Twitter: @ChicagoPhotogr

With a passion for the vast qualities of light and a complete understanding of composition and color, Adam Daniels creates photos that go above and beyond your expectations.

### Amy Boyle Photography
*photographer*
amyboylephotography.com
312.380.5993
info@amyboylephotography.com
Twitter: amyboylephoto

Amy Boyle graduated from Northwestern University where she received a degree in art history and marketing. Her love of art and the history behind the art shows in every photograph she makes.

### Bum Bul Bee Photography
*photographer*
312.841.7427, BumBulBee.com
Twitter: @BumBulBeePhoto

Bum Bul Bee Photography is a full-service boutique studio located in the heart of Chicago‚Äôs Old Town. Their mission is simple: to make every session fun, filled with laughter and on good days, lots of gorgeous light.

### Chip Beasley
*videographer*
2domes.com, 773.598.9545
crbeasley@2domes.com
Twitter: @2domesmedia

Chip is a writer, producer and owner of 2Domes Media, a boutique video production company. His experience includes producing web videos for CK Calvin Klein, Marchon Eyewear and Rocket Tour, LLC. He lives in Chicago with his girlfriend and a small white dog.

### Julia Franzosa
*photographer*
julia-franzosa.com, 773.342.1280
Twitter: @juliafranzosa
facebook.com/chicago.newborn
.photographer

Julia received a bachelor of arts in professional photography from Brooks Institute of Photography. After being a lifelong Californian, Julia moved to Chicago in 2010 and fell in love with the city.

# Contributors (continued)

**Kimberly Postma Photography**
*photographer*
postmapics.com
kimberlycreswell.com
773.791.5889
Twitter: @postmapics

Kimberly Creswell Postma is an artist and photographer living and working in Chicago, IL. Her photography is focused primarily on capturing portrait and lifestyle images.

**OKRFOTO**
*photographer*
okrfoto.com, Twitter: @okrfoto
312.909.7412

Oriana Koren is a wedding and event photographer. She is the owner and principal photographer of OKRFOTO, a photography collective specializing in creative, unique, and offbeat weddings across the nation.

**Oz Images Photography**
*photographer*
ozimagesphotography.com
Twitter: @ozimagesphoto

Brighid Uddyback is a lifestyle and fine art photographer living in Chicago. She loves being able to share her unique view of the world through her photography.

Thank you to our additional contributors:
Emily Prendergrast, Christina Noël, Richard W. Chapman and Carla Englof

Special thanks to our sponsor: A Part-Time CTO

# Craving Savings

Get the savings you crave with the following businesses—one time only!

- [ ] **Abbey Brown Soap Artisan**
  *free gift box with purchase of $25 or more*

- [ ] **All About Dance**
  *3 adult drop-in classes for the price of 1 (new clients only)*

- [ ] **Amy Boyle Photography**
  *$25 additional print credit*

- [ ] **Anne Boyle Paintings**
  *10% discount*

- [ ] **Ashé Therapeutic Massage, Bodywork & Wellness**
  *20% off a 60 or 90 minute session*

- [ ] **BabyDolls Boutique**
  *10% discount*

- [ ] **BC Speed Shop**
  *15% discount*

- [ ] **Bella Bleu**
  *10% discount*

- [ ] **The Best Career For Me**
  *$50 off Reginite Your Career Consultation*

- [ ] **Big Buzz Idea Group**
  *25% off day-of wedding coordination services*

- [ ] **Blocks Babysitting**
  *10% off initial placement fee*

- [ ] **Broken Cherry Boutique & Custom Apparel**
  *15% discount*

- [ ] **Bucktown Pub**
  *50% off your beverage of choice*

- [ ] **Bum Bul Bee Photography**
  *$175 digital image package*

- [ ] **CharisseM Design**
  *20% discount for first-time clients*

- [ ] **Chicago Chocolate Tours**
  *$5 off each ticket*

- [ ] **Chikahisa Studio**
  *20% discount*

- [ ] **Content Area Solutions, L3C**
  *25% off a STEMulating Experience activity*

- [ ] **The Cooking Chicks**
  *free first event or $100 off your first Chef Experience*

- [ ] **Creative Coworking**
  *$25 off your first month of membership*

- [ ] **Cynthia Ryba**
  *10% discount on 1st purchase*

- [ ] **Dalloo Designs Inc.**
  *15% off hourly rate for first project*

- [ ] **Dare 2 Care Now**
  *$35.00, 50-minute health consultation*

- [ ] **DeLightFull Life**
  *25% off first coaching session*

- [ ] **Engaging Events by Ali, Inc**
  *10% discount*

- [ ] **Enliven Couples Therapy**
  *$75 off 2-hour Relationship Tune-up Session*

- [ ] **Estate Chicago**
  *10% discount*

- [ ] **Figaro**
  *10% discount*

- [ ] **First Class Care, Inc.**
  *10% off full-time long-term placements*

- [ ] **five ACCESSORIES**
  *25% discount (online only)*

- [ ] **Flourish Studios**
  *10% discount*

- [ ] **Free To Be**
  *25% off your purchase of $50 or more*

- [ ] **Global Adrenaline, Inc.**
  *$500 off any trip booked in 2012 or 2013*

- [ ] **GO Cycle Studio**
  *Free class with $20 class purchase. Exp 1/1/14*

- [ ] **Good Karma Clothing for Kids**
  *10% off any subscription for the first 3 months*

- [ ] **The Green Goddess Boutique**
  *10% discount*

- [ ] **GREENOLA Style**
  *20% discount*

- [ ] **Heart Felt**
  *10% discount*

- [ ] **Helen Ficalora**
  *10% discount sterling silver collection*

- [ ] **Honey**
  *20% discount*

- [ ] **The Image Studios**
  *20% off any personal branding program*

- [ ] **Indigo Studio**
  *50% off first visit—a drop in class or any package*

- [ ] **Innovative Orthodontic Centers, PC**
  *10% discount*

- [ ] **The Insurance People**
  *free insurance evaluations and education*

- [ ] **Jessica Leigh Photography**
  *25% off photo products with 1st photo session*

- [ ] **Julia Franzosa Photography**
  *20% discount*

# Craving Savings

**Just Write! Inc.**
*15% off your first project or service*

**K Grace Childcare**
*$50 off each of the first 3 months of babysitting*

**Killion**
*20% discount*

**Knickers of Glen Ellyn**
*20% discount*

**Koru Street**
*15% discount*

**Ladysmith Jewelry Studio**
*10% off first purchase at the studio*

**Iara miller**
*25% off first order*

**LATENT DESIGN**
*complimentary one-hour design consultation*

**Laura Tanner Jewelry**
*20% discount*

**Le Papier Studio**
*15% discount*

**LifeStyle Physical Therapy & Balance Center**
*complimentary injury screen*

**Mac 'n Cheese Productions**
*free Mingler if male you refer attends one*

**Master Plan by Kathy Codilis**
*10% discount*

**MaZi Dance Fitness Centre**
*2 drop-ins for the price of 1*

**Megan Lee Designs**
*20% off an order of $50 or more*

**Merging Talent**
*25% off 3 months of marketing membership package*

**The Needle Shop**
*20% discount*

**Nourish**
*10% discount*

**Now Studio**
*10% discount*

**Open Books**
*$10 off a membership*

**Pixie Chicago**
*25% discount*

**RAW Marketing**
*one free month of services with 6-month contract*

**Salon22**
*20% discount on any service for first-time clients*

**Sangster Enterprises Inc**
*20% off business services and workshops*

**Sassy Moms in the City**
*1 free admission to a Sassy Moms Night Out event*

**SGJ Property Management, Inc.**
*half off set up fee*

**Shabazz Law PC**
*50% off consultation fee*

**ShopParty**
*with 3-hour ShopParty Luxe, get a 4th hour free*

**Shopping Girl XOXO**
*10% off any Shopping Girl XOXO package*

**Soaring Solutions, LLC**
*15% discount*

**The Spa on Oak**
*20% discount on any service for first-time clients*

**Spilled Ink Press**
*100 free thank yous with order of 75+ invitations*

**Spire Coaching and Consulting**
*$250 Energy Leadership Index Assessment™ and 1-hour de-briefing session ($400 value)*

**Studio For Change, PC**
*10% discount*

**Taxlink Incorporated**
*$25 off tax preparation services*

**There's an App for That!**
*$10 off of your first order*

**Think Royally Inc**
*20% off merchandise*

**Tiny But Mighty Foods**
*25% discount at tinybutmightyfoods.com/store*

**Urba Baby**
*20% off one item*

**Victoria Sdoukos Couture**
*15% discount*

**Village Paperie & Gifts**
*20% off any personalized gift item*

**Wax On Wax Off**
*10% discount on any first-time service*

**Yellow Duck PR**
*15% off a one-hour business consultation*

Use code CRAVE for online discount when applicable